Soul Energy

Soul Energy

Carmel Greenwood

RIDER

LONDON · SYDNEY · AUCKLAND · JOHANNESBURG

1 3 5 7 9 10 8 6 4 2

First published in 2000 by Rider,
an imprint of Ebury Press, Random House,
20 Vauxhall Bridge Road, London SW1V 2SA
www.randomhouse.co.uk

Random House Australia (Pty) Limited
20 Alfred Street, Milsons Point, Sydney,
New South Wales 2061, Australia

Random House New Zealand Limited
18 Poland Road, Glenfield,
Auckland 10, New Zealand

Random House South Africa (Pty) Limited
Endulini, 5A Jubilee Road,
Parktown 2193, South Africa

The Random House Group Limited Reg. No. 954009

Papers used by Rider are natural, recyclable products made
from wood grown in sustainable forests.

Printed and bound by Mackays of Chatham plc, Chatham, Kent

A CIP catalogue record for this book
is available from the British Library

ISBN 0-7126-0418-9

Special Acknowledgement

A special acknowledgement to Christopher Taylor for supplying meditations for the purposes of this book, and his input and help in compiling the information about the chakras.

We both use the techniques outlined in *Soul Energy* for workshops we give individually and together worldwide although all of the meditations, healing techniques and chakra information were developed specifically for this project.

Christopher Taylor is a psychic healer/reader, living and working in Hong Kong with clients worldwide. As well as teaching others to develop their own psychic ability through workshops and classes, Christopher does healings/readings in person, by telephone or by e-mail, and can be contacted at: healings@hongkong.com

Acknowledgements

My guides, who would not let me sleep until *Soul Energy* was completed.

Paul, who constantly surrounds me with gold loving energy.

Michael Bates, psychic healer/reader, California, who from his psychic amusement cleared abusement out of our lives by readings and classes to Christopher and myself.

Rose Ledbetter, psychic reader/healer, California, whose energy clearings have kept me in clarity, moving and growing every day.

To my father, Walter Joseph Salmon, who has passed over but has given me a feeling of peacefulness and support.

Contents

Introduction

When most of us hear the terms 'psychic' or 'healer', images are conjured up of crystal balls, gypsies, turbans and the like. It is quite amusing to see people's reactions when I tell them I'm a psychic. A lot of people expect to see someone in long flowing robes, somewhat withdrawn from the rest of society, rattling maracas over their head and taking on an old man's voice muttering incantations. Or they expect to see someone sitting on a rock or in a cave in India, naked except for a loincloth, with legs crossed chanting 'Ommmmm'. I know there are a lot of preconceptions.

For me it all began with a childhood in the rural bump-in-the-road gold mining town of Norseman on the edge of the Nullabor Plain desert in Western Australia. Growing up in the outback of Australia, I went to school with the Aborigines and they were my friends. The Abos, as we referred to them, were wild bush people. They preferred the hardship of the desert and the outback. The Abos are the world's hardiest people. The outback was certainly not a life of luxury in western terms but an extraordinary grounding experience. We played together but seldom spoke. We did not have to use our voices, we communicated telepathically. We sent pictures to each other through what is called the third eye between our eyes. We had fun experiencing this basic way of communicating and being. It seemed quite normal and I thought everyone had this ability. If one of us was sick or we wanted to meet each other to play, we did not need to use the telephone; we sent a message to each other by using mental telepathy, even though we lived miles apart.

The Aboriginal perception is developed well beyond the limitations of other cultures. Their senses of hearing, smell and sight seem to be above human standard. They see the vibrations of footprints in the sand and Aboriginal trackers are hired by police to trace criminals. They can tell from tyre marks the type of car, the speed and how many passengers were in the car. One night, for example, my father was having a few drinks at his favourite club. His car was stolen and the Aborigines saw that it was going too fast for my father to be driving it. They stopped the car, took the thief to the police station and then told the police to put the car back where my father had left it. My father did not even know it had been stolen until the police told him the next day.

I grew up seeing auras, a fuzz of lights and colours around people. At school we played games of putting our 'energy' into our teachers' bodies and watched its movement. Adding energy to one part of the body reveals how it uses energy, and therefore how healthy or unhealthy it is. We watched our teachers think and feel. I saw the 'patterns' in their auras correspond to their emotions and the colours continually change around them. I saw that we can suppress information in the body, but we can never eliminate it. The aura is a reflection of a person's entire well being. When a teacher got angry the aura became red. It was very entertaining and much more exciting than history or geometry lessons. I also noticed that when people were telling a lie their aura went static. I learnt to look at their aura and not listen to what they were saying. I knew that was the real truth.

Every cell is connected to, and in harmony with, the cosmic pulse. Children and all of us are powerful in our desire for that freedom and connection. Parents and teachers, believing they could control us for their own best interests, and the belief that 'this is for your own good', start programming us with their rules and limited beliefs. We are told we are not clever or wise. That is not true, but we take it on and it gets stuck as a belief in our body. At school I could see the gradual separation of the heart and the brain and the disconnection by the separation of the head and the heart, the intellect and the intuition, the physical and spiritual. My main thought at school was to stay in the middle, not to shine or stand out in any way and on no account to appear to be dumb so I would be picked on. It seemed that children that gave away their power to an adult or teacher were the ones that received more criticism and the more fearful they became. They were also 'up for grabs' by all the bullies in the playground. I could see control cords from controlling people into the person being manipulated or told what to do. There were also cords of love connecting parents to children in the heart.

The beginnings of my travels

When I was twelve I was walking up the street. It was 110°F in the shade and I was walking barefoot to the swimming pool. I always walked barefoot; the hot ground never bothered me or burnt my feet. It made me feel connected to the earth. It was a free and simple way of life.

I looked ahead of me down the town's red dust main road at nothing but the slag heaps from the Norseman gold mine and the corrugated iron houses in the town and I thought, 'There has to be something more than this.' Immediately I saw a vision, a picture in my head of a big city with bright lights where the streets were paved with gold. It had tall buildings with strange writing on them. There was a harbour with lots of boats dashing to and fro. It looked so seductive and inviting but I had no idea where it was or if it even existed. It was replaced by another picture of a different place. I had no idea where that was either but I now know it was Greece. My father was a gold miner and my mother commiserated with me on many occasions on how difficult life was for us. In this vision, the gold my father poured into rectangular containers from the ugly mine where my father worked was transformed and was paving the streets. This looked far more appealing than my present life.

I forgot about the visions but there was always this urge to leave my hometown and explore the world. Only three years later, at fifteen years old, I took off down that same road to the biggest nearby city, Perth. It was six hundred miles away, but it could have been Paradise for all the wonders that it held for a small town girl. The truly enchanting thing about it was the sense of freedom, because I could study a secretarial course and was then able to work two jobs. My wanderlust still wasn't satisfied, though. Far away places with strange sounding names still beckoned. It took me three years to save enough money to leave Australia for Europe, where I planned to begin a work and travel tour. On my eighteenth birthday I left on the first leg of my personal odyssey via a boat, more of a tub, bound for Greece. It was the cheapest passage available.

Imagine my amazement when we arrived in Athens and it was exactly the same as the vision that I had seen before. After Greece I went to England and worked for a year and then booked a last side-trip, a stopover in fabled Hong Kong. I thought I would stay there for two weeks and then return to Australia. But when the ship sailed into Hong Kong harbour my heart raced and I felt an intense excitement. It was the vision I had had at twelve years old. Exactly as I had seen it then. Meaning to stay for just two weeks, the British crown colony held my interest. This was it! In addition to its many physical, geographical and historical charms, the wealth and prosperity was alluring and seductive. I had arrived with just a few dollars in my pocket and after my life of scarcity in Australia I 'Wanted it All'. The high energy, fast pace of life was a total contrast to the laid back childhood and the psychic abilities of my Aborigine friends. I did not need to see people's auras to amuse me. Here it all was in full-blown colour, a vast array of the material world, so powerful and intense that I did not see the poverty and contrast. I saw only gold-paved streets.

Living in Hong Kong

A coincidence? No, my youthful vision had been pyschic energy. My spirit was consoling me at the tender age of twelve to get me through my childhood, knowing that there was indeed something else out there for me. I used to sleep outside on the grass and gaze up at the stars and ask them, what was I doing here? I did not understand. It was as if I had landed on this strange planet of earth and it did not feel very good. I was too happy, too full of life. I was punished for talking to imaginary friends and seeing coloured fuzz around people. My grandfather had said he wanted to die and so did not eat for one week. He died and yet I continued to talk to him. They told me if I continued with this nonsense I would end up in a mental institution. Others who were less psychic saw me as a benign idiosyncrasy. As I shared what he said with the rest of the family, they viewed it as an indication of increasing mental instability. Fearing I was having a nervous breakdown they punished me and that was that. I never spoke to him again.

I was often confused, I could talk to my spirit, and spirits without bodies, but no one wanted to know. The only ones that seemed to understand me were the Aborigines. They knew how I felt. They could see what I could see. My grandfather was welcome to visit and talk to me when I was with them. Why couldn't other people see and communicate in this way? Why was it bad? Some of the older Aborigines did not want to 'see' any more, brainwashed into thinking the white man's way was better. Many turned to alcohol to dim their awareness when they found they could not cope in the white man's world.

After being told what I saw and believed was wrong I closed off as well and thought psychic ability and healing was something far removed from the 'real world'. To feel safe and accepted by the mass consciousness of the society I lived in I learnt to live in two separate worlds. As a child I had a measure of simplicity and knew this was an opportunity to learn and create knowledge. My parents were ingrained with the limits of older people derived from their own life experience. The Aborigines and I, however, had an innocence that allowed us a level of forgiveness, both for ourselves and for them. We giggled a lot and the teachers thought we were empty-headed most of the time. They did not know what we could really see.

In Hong Kong I held the image of a confident young woman, never allowing this 'other side' of me to show. I concentrated on honing my mental skills. Working at the Hong Kong & Shanghai Banking Corporation was the first taste of really serious energy. Over the years I became a financial whiz and subsequently one of the first woman stockbrokers in Hong Kong, and then went on to have my own financial consultancy company. I wanted financial success and that was the only way to have it, or so I thought at the time. I was tired and serious most of the time, but put on a happy face. I felt my image had to be perfect, as I was well known. I had lots of money to spend and I was bejewelled from head to toe. I had made it. Or had I? When I got there, nothing was there! Was that what success was? I noticed that I mostly spent money when I was unhappy. What was missing? I had money and power, but I did not feel fulfilled. I felt empty.

I got bored reading all the financial material, adding up numbers and saw the illusion of all this money floating around in space. So I started to use my psychic ability to tune into the stock markets. It was more effective and more fun than reading all the research and forecasts of what was expected to happen. Just before the big stock market crash in October 1987 I had a strange feeling. Something devastating was about to happen. I felt it. One week before the crash I woke up and a voice said, 'Sell.' I phoned all the brokers to see what they thought but they all agreed that the market would go up another 15%. Okay they must be right. They knew all the answers, went to better schools and were smarter than me. The day before the crash a much louder voice woke me up, 'Sell NOW.' The voice was so powerful that I regained my trust and followed my gut and took action. I sold out shares I had purchased on behalf of my clients. Within 24 hours, the market had collapsed and many of those trapped in the debris lost everything. The experience taught me that, apart from financial savvy, intuition was imperative in the money-making business.

And on to San Francisco

After twenty-eight years of the high life in Hong Kong I wanted a change and moved to San Francisco, which was laid back and much more open to the use of psychic energy. From a private instructor I learnt different methods to integrate both the mind

and psychic abilities and to live in these two worlds simultaneously. Taking out old beliefs and pictures from the past
proved so beneficial that my life changed again. Most of the
time I had been living my life by someone else's programming
and now I could release a great deal of stuck energy.

The fast Hong Kong way of life had taken its toll on my
body and it was time to regenerate and to feel full of life
again. The more I practised and learned, the more I realized
how to deal with this extra dimension in my life and use it as
an asset. As I became more aware of my energy, and the
energy of others, the easier it became to identify my own
strengths and weaknesses. It also allowed me to identify
blockages or limitations, and to fix them more quickly and
effectively than ever before. It has immensely improved and
deepened the relationship I have with myself and with others.
I feel very comfortable asking for what I want and taking care
of myself. All the masks and pretence have gone and I am
happy just being me. I found that I had been living a great
deal of my life for other people. I learnt that when I ran my
own energy I was tuned into what I wanted to do and create,
not what others wanted me to do.

Most of my psychic friends have an incredible sense of
humour and a joy and enthusiasm for life, which is uplifting
and refreshing. I hope the information in this book will remind
you of your own extraordinary ability to heal and create, and
allow you to focus and access all your creative energy. Today
we are emerging from the repression and superstition that has
limited human thought for thousands of years. Freedom is
cherished by many and we believe that because we enjoy a
certain freedom of action we are truly free. However, ancient
inhibitions are still with us, confining most people's minds
more rigidly than prison bars and chains, depriving them of

attaining their dreams and desires. We all possess 'gifts of the spirit' and psychic energy is the key. You have within you a spark that only needs a little fanning to bring it to flame.

Finding the positive side

By using the techniques outlined in this book your true self will be reawakened: a pure, unique and loving individual who holds no guilt, judgement or worries, who is free and full of love and joy for each adventure in life. You will find you do not take in other people's insanity, judgements and beliefs and you will not give away yourself and your affinity. You will be calm, peaceful and neutral to anything that anyone tries to throw at you, be it abuse, problems, opinions, judgements, punishment, jealousy, you are 'less than', 'not good enough', 'stupid', 'poor', 'bad', etc. That is their problem and theirs to deal with. You won't have to prove you are okay, you will know that you are. You won't have to feel guilty, fight or resist them, that is just their opinion, and it is usually what they think of themselves.

I found it very freeing to realize that it was not my business what other people thought or said about me. You will even get to the stage of finding it amusing and humour helps you to release energy by non-resisting. As you laugh you don't hold on to energy. A tremendous release takes place in the body, which is healing.

When you live in the moment, you will sail through life, a free spirit with love and joy in your heart. Other people will not be able to control you. You will stand in your own personal integrity and truth, in your own centre, and nothing can touch you or bring you down.

What is psychic healing?

The word 'psychic' comes from the Greek word *psychikos*, which means 'of the soul'. We are not bodies with spirits but spirits with bodies. Healing is simply the process of restoring something to its original state of purity or integrity, or to make it whole again.

Psychic healing then, is the process of using the soul to heal yourself or others. It is about integrating your soul and fine-tuning your life. The more your energy is used and focused, the more you will begin to experience the power you have to effect changes in yourself.

I am certain that most of us have experienced times when things just seem to click into place. When everything happens effortlessly and harmoniously. The soul and the body can and do create miracles when working in unison. So why is it that we don't create like this all the time?

The soul and the body are like two sides of a coin. The soul constantly likes to create new experiences and it does not distinguish between good and bad. The soul merely sees something as a new experience, which is an opportunity for growth. There is discernment about which path to take, but very little judgement. The soul can change in the blink of an eye, letting go of the old and bringing in the new in a split second. I have seen people drop 20lb of weight overnight after letting go of a belief.

The body, on the other hand, likes to feel safe and secure. It likes to know what is going on and feel in control. It likes to create things in a predictable manner, and to change in little steps. When things change too quickly, the body goes into fear. Another aspect of the body is that it likes to categorize events and experiences and to form opinions. The body likes to relax and rest as well.

If you focus totally on the soul without nurturing and validating your physical needs, the body tends to rebel. It needs to relax and be replenished or disease will occur. Likewise, if you focus only on the physical aspects of yourself, without nurturing your soul, you end up with a feeling that you are missing out on something, or that 'there must be more to life than this'. The soul can create wonderful gifts, or it can just as easily take them away.

The more you can validate all of the parts of yourself, the more you heal yourself and become whole. The tools in this book can be used on a number of different levels, for physical, mental, emotional and spiritual concerns. They can also be used in any area of your life from business to relationships.

The extra senses

There are many different ways of sensing energy, and most people will have at least one of these senses operating to some degree. As children, we are probably most in tune with these innate abilities, but they are rarely encouraged or validated. As we 'grow up' we learn to put them aside and instead concentrate on what can be touched and seen. However, the more we use these abilities and integrate them into our daily lives, the stronger and clearer they become. As we explore our 'extra' senses in greater depth there are a few things that will help us along.

Clairsentience is the ability to feel energy, usually on an emotional level. This is probably the most commonly used extra sense. Most people can sense pain, anger and other emotions in others to varying degrees. Some people have this ability turned up so much that at times the information they receive can be overwhelming. It is sometimes useful to be able to turn down this ability, especially if you are in an argument. I used to be like a sponge soaking up everyone's pain and emotions and taking them on as my own. I do not do that any more. I can distinguish my energy from others.

Then there is clairvoyance. The literal translation for this is 'clear seeing'. This is when energy is read by looking at visual representations or pictures. You can experience this as brief flashes or as long movies. Most people have some clairvoyant ability but few people take the time to focus and develop it.

Clairaudience is the ability to read energy, whether it be listening to energy, spirit guides, or simply hearing a communication on a verbal level. This is what happened to me when I received the news of the stock market crash.

It is possible to physically feel energy as well. Feeling shivers down the spine or goose bumps are good examples of this. Another example would be feeling pressure on the top of the head. Each kind of energy feels physically different. This ability is particularly useful when scanning the aura. When this ability is developed you can tell a lot by how the aura feels. You can feel whether the aura is well defined, or the edges are blurred. You can feel high pressure where there are blocks in the aura and low pressure where there are holes. Emotional energy feels a lot like static electricity. This is covered more in later chapters.

Some energy has a smell too. This usually occurs when a person that has passed on has a particular fragrance associated with them, such as pipe tobacco or flowers. Although not as common as the other senses, this can sometimes be used fairly effectively.

When I was visiting my friends in Switzerland I awoke to see a young girl who had passed on standing by my bed. There was a smell of baby powder. She said to tell her mother that she was okay and happy and wanted her mother to move on with her life and to be happy as well. When I mentioned it to my friends, the mother had tears in her eyes. 'Yes,' she said, 'my daughter always wore Johnson's baby powder.' She had died very unexpectedly and very young.

Psychic healing and you

Most educated people are aware that there is something called psychic energy, or soul energy, but they do not think of it in relation to themselves. They do not see it as a power inherent in them that can be employed consciously to improve their health and make them more successful.

Learning to relax and have fun is extremely important when working with energy. When things are taken seriously on an energy level, they tend to fall into resistance and everything becomes a struggle. Serious energy feels very sluggish and seems hard to move. But when humour is cultivated and energy looked at with a sense of amusement, you are well on the way to healing it. Once humour is injected into any situation the issues can be dealt with more quickly and effortlessly. Things are less of a problem. The soul likes to play and its natural state is bliss and amusement. When this state is nurtured, you will naturally increase your ability to heal and be healed.

The ability to stay neutral to different energies is also very important, as it allows you to stay detached from what you are looking at. As soon as you judge a situation as being good, you will tend to invest some of your energy into helping to create that. Likewise, if you judge a situation as being bad, you will usually go into resistance, and your energy will become serious and full of effort. So learn to stay neutral and you will accept and see situations for what they are, rather than through your opinions of what is going on. It allows you more insight and clarity and a greater ability to feed your soul with all that valuable energy.

Chapter 1

Energy is abundant

The universe is full of energy. At the most basic level of your being, you are energy. Every day you set your own energy depending on what projects you are working on. Every day you go out into the world and use your energy for creating your life. Most of us have forgotten how to connect to the limitless supply of energy around us. So to replenish ourselves, we look to others to fill us up, whether it is by looking for compliments and approval or by bolstering our egos and making ourselves out to be better than others. The search for energy can quickly deteriorate into a competition and a power struggle. Most of this occurs on a very subtle level, so it is not always obvious what is going on, but I am sure that most of us know people who are incredibly draining to be around. Likewise, we all know people who are uplifting and inspiring, who seem to fill us with energy and are like 'a breath of fresh air'. My eldest daughter always said that I was like a big sun coming home. She waited for the sunshine to appear.

This search for energy can take up a lot of time, ultimately wasting energy. It usually comes from the belief that energy is scarce. But the more you realize that you can connect to limitless energies around you, the more you will use them and the less you will feel the need to engage in power struggles with others.

Generating energy

There is a big diamond in New York that is very expensive. Why is it expensive? Because of the uniqueness of its flaw. That is what your spirit and you are, unique. Do not let anyone tell you any different. The Aborigines feel that the birth of a baby means there is another earthly body for a fellow soul. These bodies are not expected to appear without flaws. It is the invisible jewel, housed within, that is flawless. When I was born, my mother carried me home in a plastic baby bath on the train to Salmon Gums. When we arrived, my brother cried and cried because he wanted a black baby. To him, I was flawed because I was white. The grass is always greener on the other side and most of us think we are flawed and want to be perfect. However, perfect is different for each of us, we all have different views on what perfect is; perfect to one person may not be so to another.

Allow energy to move freely and effectively through your body

So become who you are and validate that. It will antagonize you until you ask what it is. Put yourself as number one on the most important list and you will have more energy left for others. When you put yourself last on the list all your time and energy is given away and then you get blamed for not being much fun and having no energy.

Instead, the human life force is an invisible current of energy that endlessly pours into the human energy system nourishing every part of the body: mind and spirit. In negativity, the body, mind and spirit suffer from energy malnutrition and starvation. However, you can teach your body to be more energy efficient and allow energy to move freely and effectively through it. This connects you to a higher destiny, releasing much more vitality and a sense of fun. To be full of life and well being, aim to be non-judgemental and neutral, have a heart as light as a feather and aim to feel fulfilled.

Energy leaks

Before I could see energy I was always mystified how I 'lost' it when my husband came home from the office. The children and I would all be enjoying our day. Giving healings, I was fully charged and flowing happy energy. But when my husband came home the whole atmosphere changed. The children became quiet and then disappeared. It was as though there was more competition and fear in the air. We would sit at the table having dinner and within half an hour I felt like Superman facing cryptonite. Cryptonite drained the energy and power from Superman and my energy level would sag and take a dive and all I could do was watch television or go to bed. On the other hand, his energy level went up and he was charged.

When I was fully conscious and could see the colours around people (see page xii) I saw that he brought serious grey energy home from his office and this permeated the whole house. When I became aware of it, I decided I was not in agreement, so I set the house to a higher state of energy and this changed the whole atmosphere. This is not to say that my husband was a bad or uncaring person. He was just not aware of energy and its effects on others. Once I had changed the energy in the house this meant that he had to stay in his grey energy or come up to that of the house. No way was I going down there to grey serious energy. It was up to him what he did, but I had taken seniority over my own space and energy and done what was right for me.

You can never change another person and you cannot give your energy away continuously otherwise you will have an energy leak. Instead, enhance who they are and then it is always the other person's choice to be where they are. Know who you are and what you want. You can whistle your energy back. Just say, 'I want all my energy back.' Break the pattern of helping everyone; it is stopping you from getting to the top. Do not engage in arguments and in the punishment game. It is like a tennis game, scoring points. It wastes your energy and keeps you from the top. Be discerning with your time.

The body is more than an engine that works only on food and water. The electrochemical energy production or reduction values are not only of your food intake but also of anything you ingest. People pollution affects us more than air or noise pollution. When you are exposed to negative energies for long enough, the result is detrimental to your health, physically, mentally, emotionally and spiritually.

The potential within

Each person has within themselves their own richness, power, glamour and kingdom of ideas about what they want to create for themselves in life. We are all free to experience this. The choice is yours: fear or love, prison or freedom.

If you are unplugged or disconnected from your infinite potential for knowledge, love, understanding and wisdom this is difficult. If you live a predictable life dominated by worry and fear and believe that you are powerless to take charge of your own destiny then you are not connected. If you open your heart and mind you connect more and more to infinity and understand that you are more than a physical body experiencing one meaningless lifetime. You are a spirit experiencing this world as part of your eternal journey of evolution through experience. You are everything and you have the potential to know everything and do everything you wish to do.

We are all free to experience the potential within

The knowledge of who you really are has been destroyed in most of the mass consciousness and people are not connected. When you understand your true nature, power and worth, you are impossible to manipulate. Only by disconnecting from this knowledge have you given away your power. We have disconnected from our multidimensional infinity and operate on a tiny fraction of our potential. In other words, we are walking zombies most of the time, asleep, or like sheep doing as we are told and following orders and resenting it all the time. When you give away your power you become a victim and do not realize your dreams.

Fear resonates at a low vibrational pattern, a long wavelength, while love resonates at a high vibrational pattern, a short wavelength. Operating from the lower astral frequency range, the mass of humanity is disconnected from anything higher. Low frequency emotions such as fear, resentment, guilt, dislike of self, condemnation and judgement keep us disconnected from our higher self and source energy. Feeling these emotions as part of our life experience is okay but to be dominated by them and pulled down by them to depression is not. When these emotions control you, the whole psyche becomes plugged into the lower dimension and you are controlled and dominated by fear and you get stuck, sick and depressed.

Your state of being affects the rest of the world. When you change your attitudes and state of being you can change the whole, as you are part of the whole; you are the whole. You have the ability to connect with your full power, wisdom and potential. But your potential is massively undermined if you only use a fraction of your brain's potential. Fear can trigger only a few of our potential antennae while love, from which all positive emotion comes, sparks into action many more of them. When you are under the spell of fear, you disconnect yourself from infinity and live life in a small shell. When you express love you connect with your multidimensional self and your potential becomes infinite because you become infinite. You reconnect with God, love, the cosmos and the ocean of vibrational energy.

Your chakras and aura

Your consciousness is a series of interconnecting energy fields. Your emotions, intellect and spirit all resonate to different frequencies, but interpenetrate each other through a series of energy centres known as chakras, or wheels of light. The word 'chakra' comes from the Sanskrit word *cakra*, which means wheel. It is through these energy centres that imbalances are passed to the mental level and physical levels.

The large electromagnetic energy field, which religious traditions call the auric field, is the same and it is generated by the chakras, the smaller internal vortices of energy. The mind is not the brain, but it is an energy field in and around the body. The spinning of the chakras creates energy and the frequency determines the colour of each chakra. The intensity of energy produced in each chakra determines the colour that dominates the auric field. To see auric colour you speed up the normal process of visual perception, just like changing a radio station, you change frequency.

Of the seven main chakras (there are additional minor ones in the hands and feet), the lower three connect us to the earth and the top three connect us to the spirit or higher self. A human being is the connection between the physical and the spiritual, heaven and earth. The balance point in the chakra system is the heart from which we express love or hatred, the highest and lowest expressions of this energy centre's frequency range. When you are expressing love in its true and purest sense – unconditional, non-judgemental love – the heart chakra opens like a lotus flower and spins very quickly with enormous power. This resonates your whole lower consciousness to the frequency of pure love and reconnects you with your higher dimensions, which resonate to that love frequency. This is the ultimate state to be in and you feel awash with love, living in pure bliss.

I can see each chakra as a colour. The first is usually red, second orange, the third radiates yellow, and the fourth green although I often see pink as well, the fifth blue, the sixth violet and the seventh chakra is magenta. Blockages appear as brown spots, green spots of envy, dark red of emotion.

The seven chakras

The **first** chakra (see over) is located at the base of the spine. It is the most primitive of the chakras and has to do with feelings of safety and security, of 'belonging' and feeling at home in your surroundings, and of your ability to provide for yourself.

Generally, when the first chakra is cleared, you find you are able to have and achieve more without feeling guilty.

LOCATION OF THE CHAKRAS

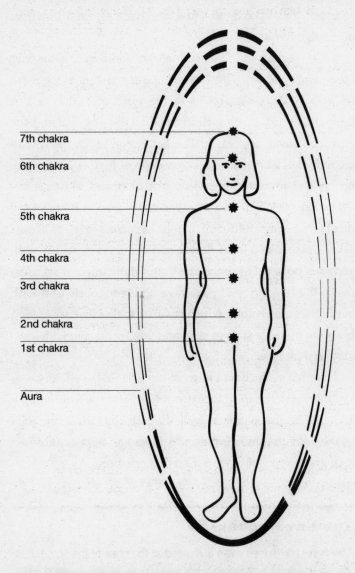

7th chakra

6th chakra

5th chakra

4th chakra

3rd chakra

2nd chakra

1st chakra

Aura

The **second** chakra is located at the navel. This chakra deals primarily with emotions and desires. It also deals with some sexual energy, especially physical and sexual attraction. Relationships generally improve and become clearer when this is cleared.

The **third** chakra is at the level of the solar plexus. This chakra has to do with how you use your personal energy and where you focus it. There is a lot of control from other people in this chakra. When cleared, you approach life from a much better perspective. You can live and create without having to control others to get what you want. You have it all yourself so do not need to take anything from other people.

The **fourth** chakra is also called the heart chakra and it regulates relationships. The energies associated with this chakra are of your ability to love others and yourself. This also has to do with your ability to integrate the various parts of yourself. When expressing unconditional, non-judgemental love, the heart chakra opens like a flower and spins very quickly and with enormous power. This resonates your whole lower consciousness to the frequency of pure love and in doing so reconnects you with your higher dimensions, which resonate to that love frequency.

The **fifth** chakra is also called the throat chakra. It deals with how you express yourself, and to what extent you give yourself permission to do this. It also has to do with your ability to communicate with others, and to listen.

The **sixth** chakra is often referred to as the 'third eye'. It is located in the centre of the head. This is the centre for clairvoyance and intuition. From this chakra you can observe and become more aware of your beliefs and start to fine-tune them.

The **seventh** chakra is also called the crown chakra, and is located at the top of the head. This is where you connect to the energies of the universe. This chakra has to do with wisdom, and your certainty about life.

Cleaning up your chakras

There is a distinction between the lower and upper chakras although in ancient sources they were not separated into 'good' and 'bad' chakras. The three-dimensional world of the lower three chakras is man's world and the three-dimensional world of the upper chakras is God's world. The fourth, the heart, acts as the transition between these worlds. As you clear your chakras it becomes evident that there exists in each of us a battle between the needs of the lower chakras and the expectations of the higher ones. It does not mean that the lower ones are bad and the upper ones are good. The idea is to integrate them and come into balance.

When energy enters your body it moves upwards from one chakra to the next. If any chakra is blocked, this energy will be blocked before it can traverse all the chakras. A healthy functioning chakra will spin and a weak chakra will not seem to be spinning at all, which blocks energy flow.

When you clean up your chakras you move out energy and old pictures of emotional events that happened to you. It is only energy, and left stuck in the body it will cause sickness. You delete programs on your computer when they are outdated, why not delete old programs you have which no longer serve you?

With more energy moving through the system you will look and feel younger and have vital and radiant energy. When the frequency of the energy gets faster your state of being becomes more refined and subtle, less physical. When you run your energy you get a warm, tingly, spacey feeling.

Exercise for physical and financial security

◎ Feel the emotion of insecurity. Just sit with it and feel the knots in your stomach and the fear it generates.

◎ After five minutes feel a dose of well being and imagine golden suns coming in from the top of your head. Feel the relief from the oppressive feeling of fear. Love feels much more uplifting.

Live an enchanted life full of energy and vitality

After giving workshops, I have become clearer and clearer in my thinking and energy fields. It is as if a dark grey cloud has lifted. People are starting to awaken to the knowledge we used to have, and we are all becoming more sensitive to the energy around us. We begin to realize just how much pain there is in our jobs and our emotional life. So how do you create a new life for yourself?

When you take time to create changes within yourself, you can direct your own path. You will not be the victim of what other people want for you. You as a spiritual being are your inner power and voice. Ask yourself, are you conscious? Are you creating with awareness and intention?

Are you letting the outside world determine what is or is not possible for you? Maybe your parents, your boss, your spouse or significant other, or the economy and society have more to say about how you lead your life than you do. Are you letting life lead you?

The real reality is that everything has a spiritual origin. You are spirit. You have unlimited potential when you tap into the spirit within. You can create your life for you. You really are in charge, and when you are leading yourself more consciously, then you are directing your own path. You owe it to yourself.

Why are so many of us living in a mental and emotional prison cell of conformity, outside of which it is fatal to tread? To buck the system puts you on the outside. Fear of being an outcast and different serves only to keep you in the system. It takes courage to let go of things, people, and sometimes but not always, families who tend to keep you trapped in the system and who do not serve you any more.

On each person's shoulders is the freedom to have his or

her own style. The art of being yourself does not waste your energy. Being afraid of the judgement of others does. Say what you think, do what you think, write what you think. People want excitement, glamour and dreams. The art of transformation, where materials can alchemize into forms, allows people to feel they are stepping into their dreams. Dreams of being able to provide this alchemy on a big scale.

To remain sane and in charge you have to remain in your own energy field. If you don't run your own energy someone else will. Do not read in the fear-based newspapers of all the horrors and disasters happening in the world. It is a good idea not to look at the news on television, when it contains so much negativity and violence. Have you noticed how the school killings get full coverage? Keep your house protected with a positive energy flowing through it and you. You have to choose between love and fear; it is as simple as that. If you choose fear, your whole nervous system is in tune with it and you will attract to you the very thing that you fear. If you choose love and tune into love that is what you will attract and receive in your life.

> **It is not your problem what other people say about you**

It is important not to listen to other people's criticisms and judgements of you. Why? Because their comments are rarely about you personally. It is not your problem what other people say about you! Their judgements are coming from their own inner being and their own pictures of how they see the world and how they think it should be. When you stay in your own energy field and run your own energy you can see very clearly that it is only their opinion and they are entitled to it, but let it stay with them. It cannot effect you if you do not allow it to.

Chapter 2

Become grounded and centred

The earth provides you with all of the things a body needs. It provides food and shelter but much more than this, it provides a place for your spirit to play and experience life. As a spirit, you are in a state of constant bliss. You are connected to the abundance of the universe, and have access to a wealth of information. So why would we want to live here on this planet? For experience! As a spirit, all the information you have is merely a concept. Creating a body and living on this planet allows you to gain practical experience, which in turn becomes part of your being. This planet is your testing ground if you like.

Ancient cultures had a strong respect for the earth. It was treated as the provider of life, and was usually referred to as

Mother. In recent history, especially in the developed nations, the earth has been seen more as something to be exploited. As people start to take an interest in the older cultures again, the connection we have with the earth will hopefully be nurtured once more. But for now you can start to explore the earth energy right away and for that to happen grounding is vital. If you don't run your energy, someone else will run it for you. In other words if you do not take charge of your life someone else will. If you live your life for someone else, when you die you will see their life flash before you, not yours. For example, if you continuously live your life with your mother telling you what to do all the time you won't achieve your own personal goals of what you came in as a spirit to achieve, nor will it be easy to have a relationship.

Much of the body's connective tissue, which is responsible for carrying electromagnetic energy, is in your legs and buttocks. If you are 'cut off' below the hips, a lot of the system that should be feeding the internal organs may not be giving you the vital energy, the life force that you need to get through life. Most white people, because of the way we think, have their legs cut off from the rest of their body. Aurically, we live in our heads most of the time and do not pay attention to the lower areas of the body. The Aborigines do not, however. They are very grounded.

As a child living in Australia I had a real problem with this and I was totally disconnected when I followed my parents. The problem lay in that the white people felt they were intellectuals and viewed themselves as being 'above it all'. They were definitely superior to the Aborigines, or so they certainly thought. It was published in a newspaper that 'the Aborigines constitute a low type in the scale of humanity.' The gulf between Europeans and Aborigines was hard to bridge because most of the Aborigines were non-literate and had no desire to work hard for material success. This was a great disadvantage to them in the new situation of the white influx of people who put their whole way of life under threat. They could not fathom why they should buy phones when they did not need them, they talked telepathically. Why buy houses when they could live abundantly in the bush? The Government bought the house I grew up in as a child to house Aboriginals, but I found it amusing to see that they slept in the yard and used the house for storage. Their oral tradition served them well when they had control of their own affairs; but when their communication lines were blocked in almost every direction, they were in danger of losing their whole heritage, including the repertoires of myth and story.

I loved going walkabout with them and listening to their tales. I never had to pack a lunch box as they knew when fruits and vegetables were safe to eat and when they were poisonous, how to gather them, and which ones had to be cooked to be rendered edible. They knew where to find water, which plants and animals stored drinkable fluids that could be utilized in times of need, and which animals and insects were good to eat and where to find them. They adapted and learned to live in harmony with the land and its seasons and with the plants and animals that inhabited it.

Aborigines have lived and roamed in Australia for at least 40,000 years and maybe longer. I saw that the intellectual approach of the white man to being superior put them into this disconnected way of thinking that is a 'cut above' the Aborigines and any poorly educated people. What I saw was that the whites had energetically 'cut off' the bottom part of themselves. When I saw how much energy and power, both physical and spiritual, was located in the legs and thighs, I could see it was a very serious problem. I was born white and tried to be like the white man but always kept my connection to the earth by walking bare-foot. When I was told to wear my shoes and stop acting like an Aborigine my legs hurt and were in pain. I had cut off the earth energy and became ungrounded. I was confused because the doctors were the ones in power, 'who knew' and were paid for knowing. They thought I had polio.

The Aborigines were looked down on so their way of grounding and living didn't fit into what I should be doing. Try as I might to adhere to my parent's way of thinking I always had this dichotomy to deal with. The Aboriginal body and spirit were con-nected as one, they had a real openness and simplicity that allowed their dreams to have mean-ing, visions came easily and their healing ability was natural. They were earth people connected to the earth and I felt spiri-tually validated when I was with them. I was connected to the stars and planets and knew who I was. At home I felt discon-nected and invalidated by my mother who said that this was all wrong and something was wrong with me. I went barefoot most of the time and when I had to wear shoes I took them off whenever I could and still continue to do so as soon as I come in the door. The earth energy solved the problem of polio and tired legs. It was not polio only lack of energy flowing through my legs and body.

Grounding offers a way of healing stuck energy

It is amusing to note that my eldest son does this as well. He was born in Hong Kong and grew up in the city with his own personal amah, a nanny, who dressed him up to the hilt each morning and paraded him off to the entire neighbour-hood. She called him 'little master', and 'little master' was her pride and joy. However, when he was nine years old I took him to Esperance in Western Australia where my parents had retired to, for six months to attend school. My mother and husband insisted he put on his shoes to go to school. He protested and always a battle and control drama arose but he was made to conform. I was very amused as I watched him because as soon as he was out of view of the house he would take off his shoes, put them into his satchel and continue to walk barefoot to school. Many of the children went barefoot in those days. Old patterns remain with you and are passed to your children, whether you verbalize them or not.

When I gave inner child workshops for children, I realized that many children from cities had never put their feet in the earth. I had them take off their shoes and walk in the mud. They cried and said they were not allowed to do that. It was dirty. One poor child in Hong Kong had his amah trailing behind him and she did not like the fact at all that I, this foreign devil, as the Chinese called the English, was making her 'little master' walk in the mud. I banished her from the class and introduced him for the first time to a connection to the earth energy. He grimaced and cried but later actually had a peaceful look in his face. It is so sad that so-called sophisticated people think that this is correct. In adult classes, the beautiful Chinese and Korean girls were also horrified at the very thought of getting their feet dirty. In big cities we become very ungrounded. Most of us in Hong Kong were living in apartments, many of them up to 35 floors high. New York and London are concrete, but do have parks. It is all too easy to become ungrounded and cut off from nature.

Grounding offers a way of healing stuck energy. That is what I was doing walking barefoot everywhere. It is a way of letting go of stuck emotions, thereby allowing the body and spirit to feel more joyful, full of vitality and giving space for the creative energy to come through. It can help to prevent illness from occurring before it becomes stagnant energy and a problem to the body. It is a way of pulling back energy from being scattered in different projects, places and people, and bringing your energy into the moment.

The properties and uses of earth energy

The first thing you will notice when working with earth energy is that it is coarse and heavy. It is a very solid form of energy and it helps to make things seem a little more real. It makes the body feel very safe and secure.

When you connect to the earth, many things start to happen. First, you are able to align your energy with that of the planet. This helps you deal with the things you want to achieve on a physical level. When you are grounded you are focused on what is happening here and now.

I'm sure most of you have had days when you are preoccupied or have things 'on your mind'. You have conversations with people, but in your thoughts you are somewhere else. This is a fairly good indication that you are not grounded. If you take a few minutes to establish your connection with the earth again, you will find your energy comes back, and you get to participate in your life to a greater extent. Since you are more focused on what is happening around you, your memory of these events will also improve.

Part of the reason you feel 'scattered' when you are not grounded is that your spirit is out of your body. The spirit moves at the speed of light and can achieve things a great deal faster than the physical body. The scattered feeling is that of your spirit running around working on projects for you. It could be finding out how your friends are doing or arguing with your boss. It could be planning your next holiday.

Meditation for running earth energies

Here are some ways of exploring the properties of earth energy. Remember that there are two energy channels that circulate energy throughout the body. The channels run down the back of the spine, loop around and flow up the front of the spine, connecting to each chakra in turn. Energy always flows down at the back and up at the front. This is meant as a guide only; it is much more important to find out what the energies means to you.

Practise running your energy regularly. A few minutes at a time may be all you can manage at the beginning, but stick to it and try to extend the time of the meditation every day a little. You should notice the results in a few weeks.

☺ Now I know how to ground while wearing shoes and living in the city. When my energy has taken a dive and I feel so serious, I am far away from smiling or having fun, then the best way to find amusement is to ground. Close your eyes and create a grounding connection from the base of your spine to the centre of the earth. Say hello to yourself inside your head.

> Connect with the earth to bring energy back to your body

☺ Funny things help us find amusement but it is actually a vibration of energy, not a joke or something funny. Put together a ball of energy that represents amusement and look to see if there are any colours or symbols. Bring the bubble of energy down into the top of your head. Let the colour of that energy float though your body.

☺ Then imagine an earth energy that comes from the earth itself and enters your body through your feet. Bring the energy through your ankles, knees and into the core of your body. You can take back your power and affinity. The body needs a little earth energy but it does not need a lot. Later I explain how to draw in just enough to satisfy your needs.

Connecting with the earth helps to bring your spirit and all of your energy back to your body. The process of connecting to the earth helps to pull your energy into the present, where it is of most benefit to you.

When you have all of your energy back in one place, you become very attractive to others, both on an energy level and physically. People may not be able to put their finger on it, but most people do notice that something has changed. You will have a lot more charisma and that certain *je ne sais quoi.*

The earth can provide all of your physical needs, including healing. Earth energy is very good for healing physical wounds. Because of its dense nature, it is also very good at setting boundaries between you and others. Being 'grounded' is also a way of checking in with the planet. It seems to help orchestrate your life so that you are in the right place at the right time, and meet the people you need to meet.

Just as the earth is constantly changing, so are you. The earth is in a constant process of growth, decay and regeneration; your body is in constant flux as well. Each day your thoughts and beliefs change, and your direction may alter. Your job may change. You may move house or move from one country to another. Friends come and go. The more you can connect to the earth and have a constant flow of new energy coming in, the faster and more easily you will be able to let go of the old and adapt to the new. Things will seem to flow more naturally.

Remember that your relationship is symbiotic with the earth. What seems like old or dull energy can be regenerated by the earth and transformed to provide new growth. Being connected to the earth is similar to grounding an electrical circuit. It means that even if the energy equivalent of a lightning bolt hits us, most of the energy gets transferred down to the earth where it can be dissipated. It keeps the amount of energy we deal with in the body down to levels we can manage. When you are connected you will find that you are not 'bowled over' by the energy of others, and can stand up for your rights and yourself more easily and effectively. This is quite an advantage in the world today and any obnoxious behaviour coming towards you need not have any effect. From being drained and afraid of this energy in my previous years I can now stand my ground and observe, 'Oh Joe is running obnoxious energy'; 'Oh Jill is running anger.' I don't get blasted and affected or wiped out any more.

As you can see, being connected to the earth has a great deal of benefits. Many types of meditations concentrate on offering your energy up to the cosmos, while completely ignoring the energies of the earth. These types of meditation can greatly increase well being, but I have found that without earth energy it is hard to bring the information or lessons you have learned back into the body and to integrate them into daily living. Earth energy helps to step down cosmic or universal information into a form that is more practical for use on this planet.

When you are running earth energy, the communication between your spirit and your body is greatly increased. This means that you can start to create a partnership between the spirit and body, where both sides work in unison. The spirit can learn the lessons it needs to learn, and the body can be nurtured and have some fun.

Finding your centre

Everything starts from the inside and everything has a spiritual origin. You can tap into that source of power within you and the bridge to your spiritual origin in your meditation practice, which puts you in communication with you as a spirit, your source of power.

As you start to communicate with yourself inside, and change from within, you can create changes on the outside. This is your spirit–life connection. Your inner work directly impacts how you live and create your life.

In the beginning it is fine to focus directly on the areas of your body you are looking at. This is usually considerably easier for the beginner. But as you progress, begin to read from the centre of your head, or your sixth chakra. Initially you may find that you need to clear out various kinds of confusion and blocks to find what you really want, not what others want for you. You will then get in touch with your own information and become truer to yourself. You will find that you do have choices and you can become a happy and contented person. You will find your relationships improve and your money-making ability will increase. You will get in touch with your sense of your own spirituality and who you really are. You will establish your ability to work with yourself and your spiritual origin through your meditation – and it is yours for life!

> **Your inner work directly impacts on how you live and create your life**

From the centre of the universe comes non-judgement, neutrality, amusement and effortlessness. That spot in time and space is in the middle of your head, just behind the pineal gland, the third eye. From there you discover your clairvoyant, clear-seeing and intuitive abilities. The god of one's own heart can be found from within the centre of one's own universe in the middle of the head. This is a special place because it has no emotions, expectations, responsibilities, and no controlling energies, which tie you to cords of commitment. You can find that spot for yourself.

Before starting to explore your chakras and energy fields, you must get acquainted with the areas associated with clairvoyance and psychic ability. The sixth chakra, located at the forehead, is the chakra that is used predominately for reading energy. Although information and sense energy is gained through all of your chakras, it is preferable to read and process the energy through the sixth chakra. There are a few reasons for this.

Firstly, the sixth chakra is a calm and neutral place from which to view energy. It allows you to read energy and convey what you see without getting involved in it. This allows you to work with energy more efficiently and effectively. The second chakra, for instance, is an incredibly sensitive chakra, and is designed to sense emotional energy. It is possible to read the emotions of others very accurately through the second chakra, and this is what most of us do. Unfortunately, all of the information you receive through the second chakra has an emotional charge attached to it, whether it be pleasurable, painful, or even so-so. This means that it is all the more likely you will have a judgement or opinion about what you are reading, take it on, and get stuck trying to 'fix' it. You can read second chakra energy just as clearly from the sixth chakra, and with a greater deal of neutrality and humour.

Second, the sixth chakra allows you to read the information from all of your chakras in a central location, instead of jumping from one chakra to another. You relate to others on different levels depending on which chakras you use to communicate.

Third, reading from the sixth chakra allows you to keep your spirit and energy in your body. It is a place where you can view spiritual information and share it with the body. There is also sometimes a difficulty in 'stepping down' the information

Meditation for finding the centre of your head

⊙ Sit down in a comfortable chair and relax with your eyes closed.

⊙ Bring your attention to a spot in the middle of your head, around the level of the top of your ears.

⊙ Move your focus back and forth in your head until you find a spot that feels calm and neutral.

⊙ Practise moving your attention away from the centre of your head, then back again.

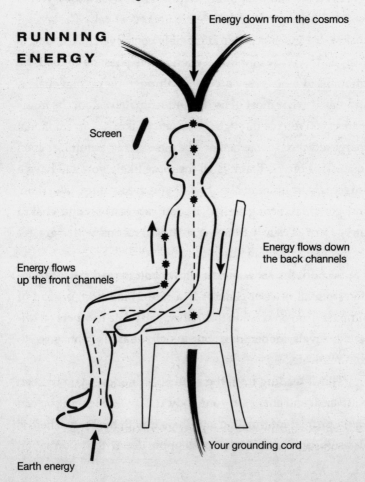

RUNNING ENERGY

Energy down from the cosmos

Screen

Energy flows down the back channels

Energy flows up the front channels

Your grounding cord

Earth energy

Meditation for establishing your psychic screen

Once you are comfortable resting your awareness in the centre of the head, you are ready to start reading energy. To do this you use a tool called a screen to view the information you are seeking.

Sometimes when you want the answer to a particular question, you will send the spirit out of your body to search for the information you desire. This method is called 'astral projection' or 'astral travelling' but while it is effective, it is preferable to read from the sixth chakra by a system known as 'remote viewing'. When remote viewing and reading from the sixth chakra, it is easier to stay detached from the energy you are reading, and the communication with the body is clearer. When sending out your spirit to gather information, it sometimes gets cluttered with foreign energy, and it takes a while to clean up.

There are several reasons to use a screen when viewing energy rather than viewing it directly. Firstly, it is a good way to make sure you stay in the centre of your head and don't intrude into other people's space. Second, the fact that you are watching energy on a screen rather than directly relating to it means that you are one step removed from it, and are more likely to stay detached from what you read. The energy on the screen is also outside your body, which is helpful for staying detached.

A screen is just what it sounds like. Most people see it as a movie screen, and it is placed out in front of your sixth chakra at a distance of a few inches to a few feet.

- Make sure you are sitting comfortably, and there are as few distractions as possible.

- Start to relax and focus your attention on the centre of your head.

- Rest your attention on the centre of your head for a few moments.

◎ If you find yourself talking to anyone or thinking of others, just quietly ask them to step back for a few minutes.

◎ From the centre of your head, focus on the area out in front of your forehead, and imagine a movie screen out there. If there is not a screen out there already, simply create one.

◎ Spend some time simply observing your screen.

◎ Notice as many details as you can.

◎ How big is it?

◎ How far is it in front of your forehead?

◎ Is it square or round?

◎ What colour is it, and what colour is the energy around it?

◎ When you are finished, open your eyes.

• •

to a level that is understandable by the body. The spirit and the body often run at different frequencies. By getting the spirit and the body to work together, you can tune these two frequencies so that they are closer together.

Once you have comfortably located the centre of your head, practise keeping your attention there for a few minutes.

At first you will probably have a lot of energy telling you to get up and do anything but sit there quietly! Don't be discouraged. This is quite normal. The more you practise focusing your attention here, the easier it will be.

The more details you can see, the more real it will appear to you and the clearer it will be the next time you go to look at it. Practise getting in the centre of your head and looking at your screen regularly, until it becomes clear and easy.

Meditation for experiencing earth energy

As mentioned previously, much connective tissue, which is responsible for carrying electromagnetic energy, is in our legs and buttocks. If you are 'cut off' below the hips, a lot of the system that should be feeding the internal organs may not be giving you the vital energy, the life force that you need to get through life.

☺ Find a comfortable chair to sit in.

☺ Uncross your arms and legs, and sit in an open position.

☺ Close your eyes and relax.

☺ Find the neutral spot in the centre of your head and focus your attention on that for a few moments.

☺ Let your awareness drift down to your first chakra. (This is located at the level of the pubic bone in men, and at the level of the ovaries for women.)

☺ Focus on the area in the centre of the first chakra, just in front of the spine, and imagine a cord of light starting from that point and going straight down to the centre of the earth. (Your cord of light may be any colour you wish; earthy colours work well, as do all of the colours of the rainbow.)

☺ Make sure the cord goes all the way through the crust, the mantle and the molten core to the very centre of the planet. When it gets there, allow the cord to root itself, forming a strong bond. Look down the cord from your body all the way to the centre of the planet to make sure it is clear. Mother earth loves this energy.

☺ Allow your body to release any old or unwanted energy down the grounding cord to the centre of the earth.

☺ Imagine energy flowing up from the earth and entering your body through your feet chakras. (Again, let it be any colour for now.)

- Bring the energy through your ankles, knees and into the first chakra.

- Let yourself relax and feel the earth energy as it enters your body. What colour is it? How does it feel? Notice as many details as you can.

- Allow this energy to rise up to the third chakra (level with your solar plexus), and let it nourish all of the cells in the body. Intend that this energy flows to all of the parts that need it.

- Intend that this energy flows until further notice, then open your eyes and stretch.

Once you have become accustomed to running earth energy and getting grounded, you can start to play with changing the colours of your grounding cord and of the energy that you bring up from the centre of the earth. You can use red one day, then try orange, yellow, and so on. Notice how each colour feels to you. You may find that some colours feel very warm and nurturing, while others might make you uncomfortable. With a little practice you will find the colours that suit you.

Running earth energy

The colours that you run (see opposite) may depend on the situation you are in and what you are trying to achieve. Instead of setting the colour of the earth energy flowing into your body, you might try intending that you receive energy that is full of confidence from the earth, or energy that makes you feel secure. Notice what colour flows up when you do this.

The properties of colours during meditation

Now is a good time to give you a basic guide as to the properties of some of the other colours used in meditation, but please bear in mind that you experience the colours for yourself, make your own discoveries, and find your own truth. Find out what the different colours mean to you. It may be the same as the outline here, or it may be totally different.

Red energy runs at the lowest frequency, and as such is the densest. This makes it particularly useful for healing physical wounds. Because of its dense nature, it is also useful for displacing energy that seems 'stuck' in your space, or pushing energy back. It is wonderful for becoming centred and helps bring you back down to earth after a hectic day. The word that best describes red energy is power. It is a wonderful validation of your right to be you.

When we become angry with people around us, we tend to run a lot of red in our auras. This is basically an attempt by the body to push the energy of those people away and re-establish our boundaries. When this is the case, you may also see blotches of energy within the red. This is the energy that is causing the anger and the energy your body is trying to break up.

Orange energy is full of vitality and passion for life. Extroverted people usually have a lot of orange in their auras. It has a very warm and validating feel, and has a wonderfully humorous quality to it. It is great for healing, as it seems to allow the cells in the body to harmonize and work together.

Yellow is great for focusing your energy and directing it for specific tasks. It helps with all kinds of mental processes.

Green has a very calm and soothing quality to it. It is the colour of compassion. It helps in healing emotional scars. It is also the colour of growth and regeneration. People who are making changes in their lives typically have a lot of green in their aura.

Blue is the colour of truth and clarity. It is a very good colour to run to enhance clairvoyance. Because it helps to get to the truth of matters, it enhances feelings of calm, as well as certainty. Blue is a very creative colour and is good for working towards achieving your goals.

Purple is a very interesting colour. It helps horizons to expand and for you to see yourself as part of the whole. It can be a very uplifting energy to run through your body, and it can be used to transmute and transform energy. The frequency of this energy is getting to the higher side of the range of the body, so take care to make sure you are well grounded while running purple energy, or you will find that your spirit will be floating above your head.

● ●

I encourage you to play with different energies, as it is the best way to learn. The more you practise, the clearer you will become as to the differences between them. Please don't be discouraged if you don't get all your answers right away. Some people will be able to sense the energies from the outset, while it may take a few weeks for others. Even if you can't feel or sense the energy right away, the energy is still running and you have started to clear out old energy. Keep at it, and the results will come!

One other thing that you may notice when you run your earth energy and get grounded is that you experience sensations of pain in your body. This happens because as you start to bring your focus and energy back into your body, you become aware of the pain in the areas from where you had withdrawn your energy. This is actually a good sign. It means that you are starting to reclaim that part of your body. The first step towards healing the pain is to become aware of it, so congratulate yourself! While you are running your energy this pain will start to break up and leave the body. Allow clean earth energy to enter the area of the pain, and let the old stuck energy flow down the grounding cord to the centre of the earth. This old energy is like food for the earth and it is easily regenerated into fresh energy. Give yourself full permission to receive this fresh energy and let go of past energies. You will find that as you continue to run your energy the pain will gradually leave.

If you feel so inclined, you may look at the area of the pain. It may be easier to stay neutral if you look at the energy on your psychic screen in front of your head, but you can focus on the area directly if you prefer.

Playfully ask the pain what its purpose is in your body. You may get information in the form of a feeling, a picture or a voice. Once you have your information, you may decide you can let go of that energy, or you may want to hold on to it and process it some more.

If you cannot get a clear picture of what is going on, don't despair. Try again in a few days, and in the meantime, when you run your energy, spend a few minutes allowing fresh energy to flow into the area with the pain, and flush out all of the old stuff. Doesn't that feel great?

Running cosmic energy

The earth has abundant energy that can be harnessed to help tune yourself to your surroundings. Cosmic energy is like food for the soul and is incredibly uplifting. It is what fills us with inspiration.

The exact ratio of cosmic to earth energy will vary from person to person. Indigenous cultures and people that work closely with the land will run more earth energy than those people who live in the cities. For now try a mix of 95% cosmic energy and 5% earth energy. You can experiment later with changing the ratio. The body needs a little earth energy but it does not need a lot. We all exist on a number of different dimensions simultaneously and you can connect with the energies of these dimensions at will.

Cosmic energy is much lighter and more refined than earth energy. It feels silky when you run it through your body. Just as earth energy is food for your body, cosmic energy is food for your spirit. Your spirit is eternally playful and the fears of the body do not affect the spirit in the same way. The spirit is merely interested in experiencing new situations and energies. It does not judge them as being good or bad. While your body is drawn to pleasurable experiences, and tends to run from some of the more unpleasant aspects of life, the spirit thoroughly enjoys both sides! The energies that you will work with from the cosmos will reflect this neutrality and playfulness.

There are infinite varieties of energies in the cosmos, and as already discussed each has a distinctive colour, feel and use. Some cosmic energies are beneficial for promoting peace and calm, while others are good for enthusiasm and excitement. But in general they all have a sense of non-judgement and ease.

In general, it is preferable to stick to the colours of the rainbow previously outlined. Many groups teach you to use white light for meditating, but there is a tendency to 'space out' while running white energy. The spirit tends to float above the head and has a hard time getting in the body, because the frequency of white energy is too high for the body to read accurately. While white light can ease the feeling of pain temporarily, it does this by kicking the spirit out of the body rather than removing the energy block. This relief only lasts until your spirit gets back in the body. You will have to deal with the block at some stage so it may as well be now. There is no time like the present!

The techniques outlined in this book are designed to create a working partnership between the spirit and the body. The colours of the rainbow help to support this relationship to a greater extent than running white energy. There are times when you can use white energy very effectively to remove the 'sting' of a localized pain, but try running gold for the moment. It works just as effectively. For general meditation, running gold works very well.

Gold energy is a very good energy to use. It is like a universal elixir that can change to any colour that the body and spirit require. It has a calming effect on the body and has a neutral feel to it. Because of its versatile nature it is perfect for when you are starting to experiment with running energy. Once you have become proficient and are comfortable with running your energy, experiment with the different colours of the rainbow. With practice you will gain a better understanding of the differences between the colours, the uses of each, and their advantages and drawbacks.

Bear in mind that there is no good or bad in energy work. It is just different. No one colour is better or worse than another. They do have different properties and all of the colours have their own particular uses.

It feels good when the spirit is above your head because your attention is not focused on the energies in your body. It is like taking a painkiller for a sore back. It may feel better, but nothing has changed. You may be tempted to put more stress on the back because you cannot feel it, which would probably lead to more injury. In the same way, if your spirit is out of the body and you cannot feel what is going on energetically, you may be tempted to take on the load of others. It may feel fine until it gets back in the body, by which time you could be loaded up with energy you would sooner not have to deal with. This selflessness is quite popular in many religions and philosophies, but in this system both the spirit and the body are validated.

The better care you take of yourself and your energy, the more you will be able to help others in the long run. Just remember to keep a sense of fun and playfulness, and you cannot go far wrong.

Meditation for experiencing cosmic energy

In this meditation, start by running gold energy from the cosmos. Feel free to change the colour and play with the different energies. You can send your spirit to play in the sea of light mentioned in the following meditation, but keep your spirit in your body by running earth energy and grounding yourself.

○ Find a comfortable chair to sit in.

○ Uncross your arms and legs, and sit in an open position.

○ Close your eyes and relax.

○ Find the neutral spot in the centre of your head, and focus your attention on that for a few moments.

○ Get grounded and your earth energy running using the previous meditation, but instead of letting the energy rise to the third chakra, have it stay in the first chakra.

○ Watch that energy run for a few moments.

○ Let your awareness drift to your seventh chakra (located at the top of the head). Focus on this area for a while. You can view it on your screen or focus on it directly.

○ From the centre of your head, imagine a sea of light, full of different energies, about 50,000 miles above your head. Take some time to look at all the energies that are available.

○ Locate some sparkling gold energy and imagine a cord of light starting from that point and coming straight down to the centre of your seventh chakra.

○ Let your seventh chakra fill up with this energy, and see the chakra start to spin.

○ Let this gold energy flow down the two energy channels located at the back of the spine, all the way down to the base. From there allow it to loop around and come up the two energy channels which flow up the front of the spine.

○ Let this gold energy flow into the first chakra, and allow it to mix with the earth energy that is flowing through. Work at a ratio of 95% cosmic energy and 5% earth energy.

○ Let the remaining 5% earth energy and 95% cosmic energy flow back down the grounding cord to the centre of the earth, where it recyles back up after regenerating in the earth.

○ Allow this mixture to fill the first chakra. Feel it fill the legs, buttocks, hips and surrounding tissue.

○ From there let the energy rise up the channels at the front of the spine, and into the second chakra. See it fill the chakra, the stomach, the intestines and the surrounding area.

○ Continue this process for each chakra in turn. When you get to the fifth chakra, allow about one-third of this energy to flow down the arms and come out of the chakras in the centre of the palms. This is known as energizing your hands and will increase your ability to physically feel energy.

○ When the energy has reached the seventh chakra, allow it to flow out of the top of the head for about two feet, and cascade down around your body, filling your aura. Make sure it flows all round you, down the grounding cord to the centre of the earth.

○ Allow your body to release any old or unwanted energy down the grounding cord to the centre of the earth with the stream of energy that is circulating.

○ Closely watch this energy circulate through your body for a few moments on your psychic screen.

○ Intend that this energy flows automatically, then open your eyes and stretch.

Chapter 3

Your pictures

When you 'read' energy, you do so by means of seeing the energy in the form of pictures. These pictures show a great deal of information in a concise and easily understandable form. They say 'a picture is worth a thousand words' and this is the case here.

In everyday life, the way you perceive each moment is represented as pictures. When you recall past events in your life you bring up the pictures of those times. When planning for the future, you do so by creating pictures of your goals and aspirations. You also create pictures of your fears.

Your thoughts, theories and beliefs can all be represented in the form of pictures. It is part of human nature to want to describe your world, to categorize your experiences and theorize as to their meaning. Pictures are how you define and set your energy. When you are about to die you see the pictures of your life pass before your very eyes. A friend, who was a pilot, confirmed this to me when he had a crash in the Hong Kong harbour. The plane did a dive and his life flashed before him. It seemed a long time but was only seconds.

For the sake of simplicity in this book, the definition of a psychic 'picture' is extended to include any type of medium for representing information. While the clairvoyant representation of energy is in the form of a picture, the clairaudient representation is vocal, such as a voice or sentence. There is still a picture associated with the energy, it is just that in this instance you have chosen to read that picture in a non-visual format. You may see a picture clairvoyantly and get a clarification in a vocal form. Likewise, you can translate pictures into any format that will convey the information clearly. It may be an emotion or a feeling, a sense, voice, picture, or any combination of them.

What you think affects who you are

We all like to have opinions and beliefs about certain subjects. It makes the body feel safe to think we have the answers and can predict what people will do and how things will turn out. The problem is that things change every second. The minute a picture is formed of 'this is the way the world is', the world will have changed and left it behind.

Ideally then, your pictures would change from moment to moment giving you constantly updated views on how you perceive things. In practice, this is rarely the case. We tend to hold on to our views far beyond their 'expiry date'.

> Update your pictures and you will be able to see life differently

By way of example, say you are involved in a conflict with someone. You have a disagreement over money, love, politics, or whatever it may be. Let's say things get heated and both parties get upset over the matter. (I'm sure most of us have either been in or witnessed a situation similar to the one described.) You are probably both nice people. You get along with others most of the time but because of the emotional exchange that has taken place, you will tend to get 'stuck' on the picture of the other being hostile. Your opinion of that person will change, as will your subsequent interactions. Every time you think of that person you will be reminded of that event and will probably try to avoid him or her, or be standoffish or hostile.

This is one incident. It is one moment in time. By holding on to these pictures or 'getting stuck' on them, you will have pigeon-holed the other person into a box and will be unable to see them any differently. Because of the way you perceive that person, your actions will be hostile or rude and will actually create that energy dynamic all over again. You will have effectively blinded yourself to the other character traits this person may possess. Until you let go of this picture you will find it hard to experience him or her in any other way. By letting go of that picture, the possibility of change is allowable. This does not mean that things will change automatically or instantly, but the chances will be increased.

How often do you take a small moment in time and use it to define someone or something? 'Oh, Peter is clumsy. He broke a plate last time he was here.' I'm sure that Peter is many things besides clumsy, but this is all we see of him.

How often have you similarly defined yourself? The pictures you have about yourself affect how confident you are, how you relate to others, and everything about you. They define you and paint you into a corner. Some pictures may be validating to you and you may want to keep them, but it is very useful to be able to get rid of pictures that no longer serve you.

When you get stuck on pictures, you trap your energy and set it at whatever the picture represents. You shut the door to the myriad of alternate possibilities and trap a part of your creative energy, inhibiting the natural flow of energy through your body. When you get stuck on pictures from the past, it is harder to accept change. Old relationships that you find hard to let go of are examples of this. The nature of the relationship has changed, but sometimes you try to hold on to the old pictures of when the relationship was thriving.

You relate to people through your pictures. Whenever you focus on an experience in your life, all of the pictures from that experience light up, as well as those that relate to that experience. It may be pictures of similar experiences or about the people involved. When you are talking with friends about a romance you are having, all of the pictures you have about romance become active in your aura, and 'light up'. If you are talking about business, you bring up all of your pictures on business.

Some of your pictures are pleasant and comforting, and some feel painful when they get lit up. When someone invalidates or insults you, the only reason it affects you is that their words have lit up those pictures in your body.

I was so glad to discover a way to find and discharge pictures quickly and effectively. Now I find it easier to use a sense of humour and even gratitude when looking at people who try to invalidate or insult me. After all, they are doing me a great service by showing me the pictures I can probably safely get rid of!

For example, some years ago I painfully discovered that the pictures I held of my daughter were damaging us both. It was my birthday and I was having a big party with friends flying in from all over the world. We had just moved from Hong Kong and bought a beautiful house in Tiburon, California overlooking the San Francisco harbour. Flowers were arriving and my excitement was increasing, then a call came from jail. My daughter had been arrested for possession of drugs and was pregnant. I had not seen her for six months as she had disappeared one day after I berated her for taking drugs. My stomach reacted and my vibration took a dive down to sympathy. 'Where are you?' I asked.

I did not know San Francisco very well but found myself in my car heading for the Mission district. After a long time trying to find the jail I went in and asked for her. I was searched and I had to leave my bag in the reception area. I was then taken to a room where I could talk to my daughter through a telephone attached to a glass panel. I spoke to myself, 'Please tell me I'm dreaming, this only happens in the movies.' I recalled *The Birdman from Alcatraz*. It couldn't be happening to me.

Work with your pictures to ensure they remain up-to-date

Well, unfortunately it was not a movie and my daughter appeared in an orange prison outfit. She was crying and was very upset and withdrawn. 'Happy birthday Mum,' I murmured to myself. My sympathy level was extreme but I was becoming very tired of these self-inflicted dramas. I could see clearly that this was another mess that Mother was expected to clean up.

She was pregnant and the father of the baby was in prison as well. I frowned. 'But it's okay,' she said, 'I told them that you would adopt the baby.' I gasped, 'Oh, thank you very much. Did anyone ask me? I have five children and I do not want a heroin addicted baby whose father is in jail coming around to my house thank you.' She was stunned. 'You don't want my baby? You have to get me out of here, please Mummy, please!'

My stomach was churning, my eyes were burning. How

could I take her home with a hundred people coming the next day and wondering what she would do. I quickly replied, 'I'll deal with it after my birthday. You will have to go to court and they'll ask for bail, I guess your dear sweet boyfriend won't pay it. Here we go again muggins.'

It did put a damper on my birthday but through gritted teeth I was determined to enjoy it. I did, however, pray for someone to teach me how to detach from her. This was destroying my family life with my younger children, and my health. It was a typical example of co-dependency and allowing someone else to run my energy and my life. Every time she took drugs I could feel it in my body. We were so connected that I felt my energy draining away trying to save her all the time, taking in her pain, preventing her from suffering consequences and feeling her own pain.

At my party there was a young man with whom I immediately formed a close bond. He was my eldest son's age but we were of similar vibration. He wanted me to talk to and teach his mother to have some fun and we talked about energy and cords and how I had to separate from my daughter. He introduced me to Michael Bates, a psychic reader, who could see it all clearly.

We laughed during the reading and pinpointed the scene exactly. I was living in a war zone. My eldest son and daughter were fighting my husband and they were all fighting in my space. I was in the middle totally confused, trying to please everyone and make it okay for everyone's hurt feelings, and couldn't think straight myself. Yes, I thought it was family life. Giving up my business and coming to California I had gone from being the chairman of a successful financial business to what was suddenly the 'Costco Queen', a housewife, not only sorting out everyone's problems but paying for them as well.

The image of one big happy family was beginning to diminish. I surrendered, I couldn't hold the 'perfect' picture of the perfect family any more. The Brady bunch won hands down, no competition.

We both laughed. There was a whopping big cord from my daughter into my third chakra and also cords going into my heart. I had not broken my agreement with her from the time she was a little girl that I would take care of her. Now she was an adult and she demanded more and more taking care of so it was time to break that agreement. I went through a process of burning the old contract I had with her and making another one. It is funny the pictures we hold of people. Even though she was in her twenties, I still held a picture of her as a little girl of two. I had to bring her up to date to present time.

Meditation for working with pictures

You have already learnt how to visualize different energies and their colours on your psychic screen. Now practise visualizing different things on your screen to help develop your psychic faculties. Try visualizing yourself, people you know, places and objects around the house. When visualizing, look at every detail.

Once your pictures have been found and identified, the next step is to start to dissipate some of the emotional charge on them. This is a wonderful exercise, as it allows you to gain deeper insight into the nature of your beliefs on a particular subject. From this you can start looking at whether these beliefs empower you or hinder your progress and make corrections where necessary.

It is not the pictures themselves that cause them to get stuck, but the fact that you have judged those pictures as being either good or bad. When you do this, you will resist the 'bad' pictures. The pictures will not be able to flow through your energy system the way they were designed to. Similarly, if you judge a picture as being 'good' you will try to hang on to it, and it will get stuck in this manner. Neutrality and non-judgement are the keys to freeing yourself. You will then have power over your pictures rather than your pictures having power over you.

Focus on validating your pictures and let the others go

- When you are sitting comfortably, close your eyes and relax.
- Find the calm area in the centre of your head.
- From the centre of your head, create a grounding cord for yourself. Allow any old energy to flow down the grounding cord to the centre of the earth.
- Let new energy come up from the earth, and into your body through the chakras at the soles of the feet. Allow it to flow into the first chakra, and watch as the circuit is formed.
- Bring down some gold energy from the cosmos. Allow it to enter your body through the top of the head and run down the two energy channels at the back of your spine.
- Let it flow around the base of the spine and up into the first chakra.
- Allow it to mix with the earth energy at about 95% cosmic energy and 5% earth energy, and allow this energy to flow up the energy channels in the front of your spine, filling each chakra in turn and spreading throughout the entire body.
- Let this energy flow out of the top of your head and cascade down like a waterfall around your body. See the energy flow down the grounding cord to the centre of the earth.
- Watch your energy flow for a while, and get comfortable with it.
- On your psychic screen, put up a picture of yourself and visualize the energy flowing through your body. In front of the body, create a bubble and inside this bubble put up a big

picture, which represents your friendships with those around you. (You may pick a specific friendship, or a general picture that represents being friendly.)

○ Allow yourself to focus on the 'friendly picture'. As you do so, let all of your pictures related to friendship light up as tiny dots of light in your aura, and watch this on your screen.

○ Let all of these dots of light float out of your body and into the bubble out in front of you. Attach a grounding cord to the bubble and let any old or dull-looking energy drain down that cord to the centre of the earth.

○ Start to look at the pictures, hear the messages or get a feeling of all the different pictures or beliefs involved. Some will be validating to you and others may be unpleasant to view. Notice which ones light you up in pain and which ones lift your spirit.

○ Once you have had a look at all of the pictures and energies involved, pick out a picture that is old or unpleasant to look at, or one that you wish to remove.

○ Create a separate bubble and let the picture occupy it. If you wish, you can allow all of the pictures with the same 'feel' to float into this new bubble. Attach a grounding cord to it.

○ Intend that any emotional charge on these pictures drain to the centre of the earth. (Emotional charge looks something like a buzzing static energy around the edges of a picture, similar to when you turn on the television without the aerial plugged in. You may see it differently though. However it shows itself to you is fine.)

○ Bring down some gold energy from the cosmos and let it wash over these pictures, neutralizing and replacing the emotional charge.

○ Intend that any confusion or resistance energy contained in the picture flows down the grounding cord to the centre of the earth, allowing gold energy to replace it and wash the pictures.

○ When you have cleaned the pictures sufficiently, you may notice that the unpleasant feelings start to leave your body, and you can look at the pictures in a calmer manner. The only thing left to do is to release those pictures, and let them fall away down the grounding cord to the centre of the earth.

○ When all the pictures have gone, let the entire bubble get sucked down the grounding cord to the centre of the earth so that the energy can be regenerated and transformed.

○ Bring down some gold energy from the cosmos, and fill your entire body. Imagine all of the cells drinking up this energy until they are full.

○ When you have finished, open your eyes and stretch.

● ●

Chapter 4

The first chakra:

survival –
fight or flight

The first chakra is the most basic of the chakras and regulates your survival instincts. It is the chakra responsible for your 'fight or flight' reflex. It determines whether you stand your ground in situations that involve conflict, or whether you run.

All survival and self-preservation is influenced by the first chakra. It is located between the base of the spine and the pubic bone. Survival, sensuality, pleasure and power and being alive is its objective. The first chakra is attracted to other first chakras, and this is how you are sexually attracted to someone.

When you get into pain, the first chakra cries for life. To recall the trauma consciously, you must achieve that expanded field again. You are then able to change attitudes and feelings that were linked to the traumatic experiences that were lodged within your subconscious. Because of their association with pain these feelings are destructive and restrictive. Locked in your subconscious they continue to influence your thoughts and beliefs unconsciously. Once brought to consciousness they can be examined and simply be released, making room for more healthy attitudes and feelings. Release is usually sudden and is accompanied by a flood of emotions. Once these old angers and fears are surrendered, old patterns give way to newer and healthier ones. Suppressed anger, fear and pain are all indications of imbalance in the first chakra.

Personal animal magnetism, charisma and power all emanate from the first chakra. When it is energized, you can dominate a room with energy and authority. Most of us withhold power in favour of humility and suppress our power by sitting on it. Without having our firepower we can't burn diseases. Power and energy is ours. Use it or you lose it. Not using power is a misuse of power. To have power is to impact everything and everyone around you. In giving from the source you open the flows that feed you and avoid depletion and burnout. You can empower others by giving them energy. You can always tap into the universal source of unlimited energy. But you must be careful not to attract people who need energy, who are needy and want you to care for them. You must be selective.

Through life experience and parental programming you pull back power and withhold it. Overt power is not readily accepted in our society. Your basic drive and ability to prosper, how well you survive, depends upon how much power you allow yourself to have; the spiritual fire that manifests matter. At birth, the spirit is fused into the body as a baby passes through its mother's first chakra. It is the fire of the energies of the mother and baby through which the spirit infuses life.

The kundalini

The kundalini is located in the first chakra and is a Sanskrit word, meaning serpent. The serpent symbolizes the subtle currents of the body and the spiral windings of the soul's evolutionary path. The female and male serpents intertwine in the body and the source of energy flow moves from chakra to chakra up the spine. In the kundalini experience, one is aware of all the chakras awakening and the energy flowing freely between them.

The kundalini rises to centre around and stop near the pineal and pituitary glands, which are very close to the thalamus and the hypothalamus in the midbrain (see oposite). When the serpent power is activated you can 'see' without any physical light. You can see and sense and feel the inner invisible world. The kundalini is the primary energy source for your spiritual vehicle. People who do not have the chakra system awakened are half-alive. They live life in a numbed state. The experience of the 'rising' or the awakening of the kundalini can make you feel so incredibly alive because more energy is available to you than you previously had access to.

After the kundalini opens, the second chakra opens and connects the third eye so that everything you feel you see. This is highly visual as the right and left hemispheres of the brain come into synchronization and you have an activated awareness throughout your body. The sensation is your life force moving through you and is very powerful. Your body and mind fill with an extraordinary amount of energy. I now feel

The pineal gland

The pineal gland is an endocrine gland found in vertebrates. It regulates the production of the hormone melatonin. In some lower vertebrates the gland has a well developed eyelike structure; in others, though not organized as an eye, it functions as a light receptor. Studies that were carried out in the 1980s suggested that the pineal gland was the evolutionary forerunner of the modern eye.

The pineal gland is located within the third cerebral ventricle along the midline of the brain. Its name is derived from its shape, which is like that of a pine cone (Latin: pinea). In the adult human, it is about 0.64 cm ('/₄ in) long and is pinkish-grey or white in colour. It weighs little more than 0.1 g. The gland is large in children and begins to shrink with the onset of puberty. In adults, small deposits of such minerals as calcium make the pineal body visible on X-rays.

The pineal gland and the area of the brain just behind it, are the areas you use to access your clairvoyant ability, and where you 'see' energy.

The pituitary gland

The pituitary gland is a small, oval endocrine gland that lies at the base of the brain. It is located between the eyebrows. It is called the master gland because the other endocrine glands depend on its secretions for stimulation. Because of this, focusing on the pituitary gland helps you to access energies that are especially useful for doing psychic healings.

- ❂ Make sure you are in a comfortable position and relaxed.

- ❂ From the centre of your head, move your focus down an inch or two and forward, towards the centre of the eyebrows.

- ❂ You may notice the gland starts throbbing when you focus on it. This is a sure sign that you are at the right spot.

- ❂ Notice the difference between the pineal and pituitary glands.

fully alive and aware on a regular basis. But before discovering the effects of psychic healing the lights were on but no one was at home most of the time. I was only half-alive. However, now my physical and psychological states have slowly changed. I had a tingling feeling on my third eye and the top of my head and could hear a buzzing. This red ball of fire certainly changed my body.

When the kundalini starts to open it is best not to resist it. This would be painful as you are resisting the energy flow that is trying to open. Allow the kundalini to open spontaneously and slowly. You should feel ripples of heat and rushes of energy.

When you are told that the rising of the kundalini will make you lose your sanity this is not true. It is the inability of a person to hold awareness on several levels of reality simultaneously that sends you nutty. What you consider psychotic is often 'ecstatic'. You may see lights and colours, hear buzzing and your body will shake. You experience two parts of yourself: the observer who silently watches you participating in life and you the participant. When you meditate regularly you learn to think on multiple channels and have a much broader understanding.

> When the kundalini starts to open it is best not to resist it

Let me tell you how my kundalini unexpectedly rose. It didn't happen in an ashram while chanting. I was a shy little girl growing up in Australia. Most photos show me sucking my thumb and twirling my blonde hair, afraid most of the time. The rage was the kundalini rising: the red fiery force that rose uncontrollably when I hit my ex-husband, who was an alcoholic. Before that time I had really been a victim of life. After that I changed considerably. I walked out the door with nothing but my Buddha. I wasn't afraid any more. After all those years of fear, I awoke and just wasn't afraid. The fear had been burnt away. It was as if my DNA had changed and I was another person. I moved from being fearful to formidable. I knew what I wanted, I got it and nothing stood in my way. I was not a wimp. There seemed to be no limitations. The thought of having to support my children had always weighed on my shoulders and pushed me forwards, but it was a stronger force than even that.

My husband always used to blackmail me that if I left him either he would kill himself or I could not take my two children and that had kept me a prisoner. But after my kundalini rose, it was as if things and people were not going to keep me from working against myself any more. Instead of fear that he might kill himself, I looked him in the eye and asked how I could assist him. Did he want me to throw him off the balcony or slit his throat? I grabbed the carving knife and threateningly waved it in the air. His eyes bulged and his broken voice called me a bitch. 'Well,' I said, 'it is about time I was a bitch.' My self-respect and preservation were much more important, whatever the cost of what I had lost financially.

It is amazing, though. I just put my head down and worked. I even had to borrow money from the bank until I earned more money. After a week, my ex-husband had changed the locks on the door so the children couldn't get in. At that time I was doing an interview all day thinking I would get more clients from the article. It was called *From Eight Till Late*. I was sitting in my stockbroking office with the journalist. A call came from him saying, 'You're having too much fun, you have commitments, I've locked the children out, you'll have to take care of them.' I had to hold the phone out he was so loud. I was shaking inside but kept my composure and excused myself. I called my lawyer and told him what had happened and asked him what I should do. He said, 'Well, we don't have to go to court to get the children back, he's thrown them out.' 'Oh, okay,' I murmured, 'good.' I quickly phoned a neighbour and asked if she would take the children in when they came home from school as I would be back after eight. I returned to my office and calmly carried on the interview. My stomach was churning and my heart pumping but I tried not to show any emotion. 'God, please get me through this day,' I said to myself. Next a hysterical call from my maid. He had thrown her out as she was accused of helping me. I told her not to worry. I would somehow replace her things. Just wait for me.

Well, the journalist did not know what to make of all this but we carried on through the day. He was taking photographs of the office, lunch with clients and then we went to a radio studio where I did a weekly radio show talking about how to make money. People phoned in and asked advice. It was a good source of clients. After that I took the journalist on my friend's boat and he took photos of me scuba diving. All I wanted to do was get my children but we made it through the day. I had managed to phone them and reassure them that I would be there after 8pm to collect them.

As my ex-husband was a high-ranking officer in the police force, people were afraid of him and as his position was a position of authority they listened to him. He threatened me that he would see me in the gutter where I belonged. He would see that I was kicked out of Hong Kong, penniless and alone. He would keep the children. He then went about arresting a good client of mine. He took him in for questioning and threatened him. The poor man quickly withdrew his money, which I was managing, from his account. He phoned other clients but somehow through all the chaos, I managed to get through. I had never experienced harassment before and no one would believe what was happening, I was totally alone. It was very wearing and hard to accept that a man I had loved and who was the father of my children would do this to me. It was very humiliating and sad, but I kept my composure and never said one word against him.

I had an inner strength and resolve that kept me going. I was alone but did not feel alone, I felt connected to the divine. So-called friends that I had entertained for years, deserted me and it was an uphill struggle. He wouldn't give me any of my possessions but 'a voice' said to me, 'Don't worry, let it go, they are only things, your self worth and energy are more important. You don't have to get anything from him or punish him; God will take care of him. Everyone finds their own level and gets what they deserve.' I was upset at the time that all I had saved for was in his house but was reassured by 'the voice' to let it go, I would be taken care of. Later my ex-husband went to pieces and was given early retirement and sent back to England. From being an acting assistant commissioner of police, with all his constables saying 'Yes Sir, no Sir, three bags full Sir,' this was a difficult transition from being very powerful to one of power-lessness.

'The voice' was right, and I am so glad I listened to it. I did not have to do anything. God took care of it. My life took a dive upwards financially and emotionally and his life really went down the tubes. I don't know about ending up in the gutter, my life was gold-paved from then on. I went on to open my own financial company.

Be yourself

The fight or flight reflex does not only occur on a physical level, but on an energy level as well. The spirit does not like pain, and one of the ways the spirit deals with this is to withdraw from the affected area, or leave the body altogether. Through the techniques in this book the spirit is taught to get back in the body and to stay there when pain occurs. In this way energy is processed and cleaned up faster, leaving more and more room for creativity and vitality. So a healthy first chakra is essential for creating an atmosphere where the spirit feels safe enough to stay in the body and feel secure.

The first chakra is also the place where you connect to the earth. This is where you create a sense of belonging on the planet and of fitting in with your surroundings. It is where you set your energy for life on the planet, and it is through your first chakra that you exert your right to 'be' yourself. This is where you take the infinite possibilities and make choices as to how you will run your own energies.

The first chakra deals with all of the energies of survival. Humans do not have many natural predators these days, only the financial sharks, and on the whole life has become safer as we have become more technologically advanced. Nevertheless the first chakra still has its work cut out.

More than just making sure you don't get shot or wander into dangerous situations, it is concerned with putting food on the table, bringing in income, protecting the family and those you love. It is concerned with sustaining you physically on the planet. It is common to see parents (especially mothers) and children connected with cords running between their first chakras. This is basically protection energy, and an agreement for the parent to take care of the child, and to be responsible for their safety and well being.

Occasionally this will happen with others as well, whether you feel you need to be taken care of or need to take care of someone else. While it could be considered a noble and selfless gesture to help someone out in a time of need, and it is nice to receive a helping hand from time to time, the underlying messages can be invalidating. When one person depends overly on another, the underlying message is that they cannot create for themselves. There are payoffs on both sides of this game. The helpers get to feel superior, and get to validate themselves for being 'good'. The people receiving the help have someone to help them create. They can remain lazy while someone else takes responsibility for them and they can blame you for doing it wrong.

It is not necessarily a bad thing to want to help others or to receive help. It is a part of life and occurs naturally. Sometimes, however, you will get 'stuck' in one role or another. The more you work on these energies in the first chakra, the freer you are to play both these roles at the appropriate times. The more you release your pictures, the more you get to decide when you want to help others, rather than having it be a duty. Being psychic is primarily about being aware of what your energy is doing and where it is focused. When you gain that awareness of the games you are in, you can consciously choose which role you want to play, or if you want to play at all, rather than have your choices on auto pilot. It is also interesting to look at whether you have asked to be 'helped', or whether someone thinks they know what is good for you more than you do.

> Let your first chakra run freely and you will have an air of calm and focus

When a person is grounded and has their first chakra running, they have an air of calm and focus about them. People are naturally attracted to this and there is a tendency for people to want to ground their energy through you. This basically means that people want to 'dump' their problems on you, or get you involved in making decisions for them. This is one of the first things you will encounter when starting to run your own energy. The clearer you become, the more you will be able to see this happening, even on the subtlest levels, and decide whether that is something you wish to engage in or not.

Freeing yourself from taking responsibility for others does not mean that you should never give people a hand. It simply means that you give yourself choices as to whether you help or not, and feel okay with yourself, whatever choice you make.

The purpose of the first chakra is awareness of your own life force as it moves through you and your connection to the force that creates and maintains life through the universe.

Meditation for experiencing the first chakra

⊙ Find a comfortable chair to sit on.

⊙ Relax and bring your attention to the centre of your head.

⊙ Get grounded and get your earth and cosmic energies running (see Chapter 2).

⊙ Watch your energy running for a minute or two.

⊙ Focus on the first chakra. (You can do this by focusing directly on the chakra or by viewing it on your psychic screen. Try it both ways and familiarize yourself with the difference between the two methods.)

⊙ Notice as many details as you can. What does the chakra look like? What colour is it? What does it feel like? Does it feel strong and vibrant or does it feel heavy and dull? Does it hurt? Is it spinning freely? Do you have thoughts of other people when you focus in?

⊙ Observe your chakra for a few minutes without judging what you see. Get used to the 'feel' of your first chakra.

○ Either on your screen or in the chakra, focus on all of the people who are trying to save you. (You can get the information by seeing it on your screen, by hearing them and saying hello to them, or by any method at all.)

○ One by one ask all of these people why they are there, what they are trying to save you from and why they feel the need to save you. Get as much information as you can from these people. (It may be that some of the people you see have passed away. Just because people have passed on does not necessarily mean they have let go of us!)

○ Thank all of these people and fill up with liquid gold energy.

○ Focus on all of the people you are currently trying to save. Who are they? Why are you trying to save them? Is it because they have asked for help or because what they are doing is 'lighting up' your own fears?

○ When you are done, fill yourself up with liquid gold energy and open your eyes.

●●●

Chapter 5

The second chakra:

emotions and desires

The second chakra is the seat of the emotional body where all emotions are processed. You can sense what others are feeling. It is very important for women, as this is where we create babies.

The second chakra is located at the navel. It is the chakra of the emotions, desires and the chakra that aids you in setting boundaries in your relations with others. It is where you can 'feel' the joy or pain of those around you. You do this by bringing information into your body to process it 'in house'. When you do this, however, the distinction between what is your energy and what is someone else's gets blurred. As a psychic, it is important to be able to set effective boundaries as to what energies, if any, you want to take on. Later on in this chapter, you will learn how to change the amount of energy you process through this or other chakras.

Facilitating at inner child and energy workshops I was shocked to see how repressed this chakra was in many people. The beautiful Barbie doll girls and Southern belles who were so sweet that butter would certainly not melt in their delicate mouths let loose with a vengeance when allowed to do so. They would come in and say that their lives were 'just perfect' and then it erupted like a volcano. The venom and snake and spider energy was high voltage to say the least.

It was the upper-class Victorian British gentry that decided and believed that emotions were bad. The English saying of 'do not open the can of worms' (you don't know what will come forth) still applies. 'If you do not talk about it then it does not exist.' Do not show pain or anger; just 'bite your bottom lip.' This totally disfigures and annihilates the second chakra and unbalances the whole body. But when these lips are allowed to open, the repressed rage and anger comes out like a fire of hot energy, the flame of freedom. The body is so thankful and relaxed. Emotions are healthy and certainly not bad. It is the misuse of emotions and the resulting sickness and imbalance this creates in the body and life that is bad.

> With the second chakra you sense what others are feeling

When you look out at the world through the second chakra, the tendency is to attach an emotional charge to everything you see. On an emotional level you will feel good or bad about certain circumstances, and derive pleasure or pain from them. This helps you decide what you desire when faced with choices. The energy in this chakra is usually set one way or the other. It may be close to the middle, but there is usually a preference of some kind.

Those of us who are 'too sensitive' usually have highly developed second chakras and tend to process our information on this level. When the second chakra is fully open, the emotional information can be so overwhelming as to swamp you and affect your moods. With this amount of information coming, it is hard to distinguish your energy from the energy in the surrounding area. It is as if the energy of others overrides that of your own feelings and you will 'match' their energy. When you have this chakra wide open, it is easy for people to make you feel bad or to lift your spirits, and life can be a bit of a roller coaster ride. But when it is turned down slightly you can read the information at a level that your body can process easily, and start to have more say in what energy you will take on. With practice you can learn to close this and other chakras down to a more manageable level where you can still read the energy, but it does not affect you so deeply.

The second chakra aids you in making choices based mostly on whether similar situations in the past were pleasant or not. You will tend to head towards things that give you pleasure. When your chakras are wide open, however, it can be hard to distinguish your energy from that of people around you. Sometimes, when someone around you is particularly passionate about a certain subject, you will be carried away by his or her enthusiasm and will be more than willing to invest some energy into helping create their vision (as long as you can soak up some of that enthusiasm!). This energy rush feels great, but it can distract you from your path. When you have your chakras turned down to a more manageable level it becomes easier to recognize their passion as their passion and not yours. It then becomes easier to stick to your path and to create passion for your own desires.

Meditation for adjusting the level of information received through a chakra

Here is a good place to introduce a psychic tool called a gauge. It creates a good visual representation of what is going on in lots of situations. It looks just like the fuel indicator on a car with empty on one side and full on the other. Thinking of a scale of 0 to 100 is usually better though. Close your eyes for a minute and create a gauge in front of you.

○ Find a comfortable chair to sit on.

○ Relax and bring your attention to the centre of your head.

○ Get grounded, and get your earth and cosmic energy running (see Chapter 2).

○ Watch your energy running for a minute or two.

○ Focus on the second chakra. (You can do this by focusing directly on the chakra or by viewing it on your psychic screen.)

○ Observe your chakra for a few minutes without judging what you see. Get used to the 'feel' of your second chakra.

○ Either on your screen or in the chakra, put a gauge up for how open the chakra is. See, hear or feel the answer as a number between zero and one hundred. (It may be that the number changes or you get two numbers. That is fine. This will tell you the normal range of how open it is. The chakra will open and close, depending on the situation.)

○ Imagine a psychic hand reaching out and turning that gauge down to about 10% open. As you do this, notice what comes up for you. As you change the settings in your body you may hear or get a sense of other people. These are the people that this change is affecting, and some of them may not like it. Playfully ask them to leave or ignore them for the moment. This is your body. You do not have to get permission from anyone to change your own energy.

○ Create a huge ball of gold energy above your head and allow this gold energy to come down and fill your entire body. When you are done, open your eyes and stretch.

Experiment by opening the chakra as wide as it will go and noticing how that feels, then turn it down slowly 5 or 10% at a time. Stop for a few moments at each level and feel the difference as you turn it down.

Permission to experience the full emotional spectrum

When we were children we had a great deal of permission to experience the full range of emotions. When we were hurt or felt pain we cried; when we were having fun we laughed. As we grow up, however, most of us are taught to repress our feelings and we are told that some feelings are not okay. 'Big boys don't cry', 'Bite your bottom lip' or 'It's not nice to be angry.' We are taught to keep our emotions bottled up and show a tough face to the world. But when you repress and resist your emotions it is easy to get stuck and clog up your energy system. Most people will try to funnel the energy into a different form, like feeling upset and hurt about the actions of another, then turning that into anger, resentment and hatred towards the person involved.

Allow yourself to feel so your emotional body will function more effectively

In order for your emotional body to function more effectively it is beneficial to allow yourself to feel again. One sure way to deplete your energy is to resist something. You will expend a great deal of time and effort resisting feeling a certain way, when it may be much quicker and easier to feel it and let it go. When you are neutral towards experiencing different emotions you can process them with increasing ease. This is especially so when your second chakra is set at a comfortable level.

Setting your boundaries is a continuous process. It is useful to check your second chakra regularly throughout the day to start to become aware of how open it is. With practice it will become clearer what is your energy and what is someone else's. One other point that should be made is that emotions depend solely on the pictures of the individual. The same action can elicit a very different reaction from different people. While you should take responsibility for your actions, it is unwise to judge your actions from the reactions of others. No matter what you do, some people will love you for it and others will hate you for it.

A good phrase to remember is that 'it's not my problem!' If you get caught up trying to please everybody and justify your actions you will not have time for much else. If you follow your conscience and act according to your truth then you can't go far wrong.

People's actions, and all energies for that matter, are neutral. It is yourself and your perception of those energies that makes them good or bad in your eyes. No one can make you feel bad unless you go along with him or her. When you take responsibility for your own emotions, you become empowered and change is possible. When it is someone else's fault, you have no power to heal yourself.

Sexual and sensual energies

The area around the second chakra also deals with sexual energies. This is an area that has a number of different influences. In addition to your own beliefs, there are cultural, religious and family influences. A whole book could be written on this subject alone, but suffice it to say that we are sensual beings. The Supreme Being, the Great Spirit, God, Allah, Buddha or whatever you choose to call Him/Her gave us our senses so that we could use them to experience all aspects of life on this planet. Some religions and spiritual practices seek to repress the sexual parts of our beings, but I feel that it is better to get to the point where you control your sexual urges rather than have them controlling you. While letting this part of life rule you will probably be detrimental, it is a wonderful way for two people to validate each other, and is a great deal of fun as well!

Sexual union is the joining of two sacred life forces. But you must be selective with the quality of energy that you choose to merge. Many people are unconsciously 'living with the enemy', which takes away light and life. You must protect yourself from that which can harm you. Only merge with partners that bring light and life. It is very important. In choosing mates, friends and teachers look for the quality of their light, not the way they look or the ways they say who they are and what they do, but the way your body feels in their presence. Many of us choose our loved ones and friends for all the wrong reasons. If we come from backgrounds in which our parents did not carry a lot, if any, light or abused us in some way then if this is not cleared, we sense people with low energies as being 'safe'. We stay away from people who have abundant energy as people to be avoided. This is not the way to live your life if you want to maintain a strong energy system, capable of meeting the challenges of a constantly changing planet and an evolving consciousness.

I had a girlfriend who married an Englishman. He disliked me intensely and forbade his wife to see me. My energy and my personality were too much for him. During a course in a room of nearly a hundred people we all voted for the most giving and the most taking person in the room. He was voted the most taking and I was voted the most giving. He came up to me later and sheepishly said how sorry he was. He actually wanted to be as happy and outgoing as me but did not know how to, so he condemned me.

Overcoming suppressed energy

All too often people see sexuality, intimacy and power as being mostly unacceptable, whereas repression of anger and lack of vitality is acceptable. As a result, our awareness and sense of vitality and ability to touch is suppressed. This creates an energy block of suppressed energy, which stays throughout the entire life of many people who never find an outlet. But when your second chakra is open and your energy is moving you feel you are alive and tactile. You will have a powerful impact on others.

Life force itself, the creator and sustainer of energy and life, is connected to the second chakra; the emotional solar flame that ignites passions. It is the pilot light for the energy of the chakra system. The essence of fire, that sets the power in one's life. The quality of our sexuality, vital forces and drives. Our bodies are connected by vortices of energy that are connected to the Source or God. The more you are plugged into this source, the more energy you have to create and take charge of your own life. It is essential for those who want to control you that they must find ways to limit the amount of energy you have. This is where you became unplugged from the life force, which is totally free.

When you are emotionally upset and are living in fear it makes all the energy centres become unbalanced and over-loaded and you can't think straight. There is static above the head, which is seen in a reading as a milky white haze. This leads to confusion and the inability to think straight. This gets passed on to the physical body and manifests as blockages and disease.

The Church set about to close down this energy centre by saying that sex was evil. When we are worried or feel guilty about sex, the energy gets stuck in the second chakra and imbalanced. Sex is fantastic and meant to be enjoyed. What can be better than the ability to show your love in the physical body of another person? It is a gift to be enjoyed and expressed without suppression. Love is the ability to flow and not be suppressed or afraid.

In Asia they understand that the power of sexual energy can be used to create or destroy. Sexual intercourse is seen as the union between male and female, yang (male) and yin (female). Tantric sex has been used to stimulate the sexual energy held in the base of the spine, the kundalini energy. This raises the energy up and down the spine until it reaches a vibratory state that connects you to the cosmos. It is called lighting the inner fire. Once you are connected and awakened you have a constant supply of powerful energy with which you can create whatever you want. This sets you free. The Christian and Victorian obsession with making sex dirty, forbidden and wrong created a guilt-ridden experience that suppresses the kundalini energy and disconnects you from the cosmic levels of self.

However, the ability to reach orgasm requires an open and expanded state. Kundalini energy must travel up the entire chakra system to the third eye to stimulate the neurotransmitters in the brain responsible for the orgasm. You need a lot of energy for this, more than for your daily activities. Lovemaking is an exchange of energy. Sexuality is mergence with another, the quality of which depends on how much energy you can hold in your system. When you run your energy you open your channels and you have an enormous amount of energy for lovemaking. Besides giving, you must surrender otherwise there is no real exchange and no orgasm. The degree on which you can achieve sacred mergence with your partner is related to the limitations you place in that union, physical, mental and emotional.

> **Become more exquisite, open and delicate in your perceptions**

You grow in consciousness when you 'stay' in the body, stay present as the energy expands and increases. When you maintain energy you can extend orgasm. The loss of consciousness may be experienced when you go to sleep as one is pushed out of the body. The desire to make love over and over again is an indication that the open expanded state achieved in the sexual mergence has been so pleasurable, so awakening that you desire to remain in that heightened state. Good sex means having an open system capable of maintaining a high level of energy exchange.

How you access and exchange sexual energy is reflected in every other aspect of your life. It is basic to every success in life, health, relationships and business and service. Being open and present means that your kundalini energy is flowing and the level of energy exchange is high enough that you are aware of energy and experience entering your field. This allows you to push negativity out of your system, to eliminate that which is unhealthy or undesired and to keep that which is healthy and desirable. You can then recognize negativity and eliminate it from your energy field. Your goal is to become more exquisite, open and delicate in your perceptions.

Meditation for experiencing the second chakra

⚙ Find a comfortable chair to sit on.

⚙ Relax and bring your attention to the centre of your head.

⚙ Get grounded, and get your earth and cosmic energy running (see pages Chapter 2).

⚙ Watch your energy running for a minute or two.

⚙ Focus on the second chakra. (You can do this by focusing directly on the chakra or by viewing it on your psychic screen.)

⚙ Notice as many details as you can. What does the chakra look like? What colour is it? What does it feel like? Does it feel strong and vibrant or does it feel heavy and dull? Does it hurt? Is it spinning freely? Do you have thoughts of other people when you focus in on it?

⚙ Observe your chakra for a few minutes without judging what you see. Get used to the 'feel' of your second chakra.

⚙ Either on your screen or in the chakra, focus on your passion for life and your excitement at being alive. See, hear, feel or sense where you are at in respect to that. Are you blissfully happy? Is your energy stuck in misery and depression?

⚙ In the chakra, imagine a representation of yourself at that energy level. See as many details as possible. How does it feel? What colour is it? What messages do you get?

⚙ Next to that picture, put up a picture of yourself being blissfully happy and passionate about living. (You can create one from scratch or remember a time in your life when that was real, and create a picture from that.) Notice the difference between the two in as much detail as possible. Allow yourself to feel the energy of being blissfully happy.

⚙ Focus on what is stopping you from having that right now. Let the answers come without trying to work them out too much.

○ When you have received all of this information let the energy from the blissfully happy picture start to flow into the picture of how you feel today. Let the energy start to dislodge any old or stuck energy that you wish to let go of, and watch as this old energy gets flushed out of the picture.

○ Create a grounding cord on the picture and let all of this old energy drain down to the centre of the earth to be regenerated.

○ Create a huge ball of gold energy above your head and allow this gold energy to come down and fill your entire body.

○ When you are done, open your eyes and stretch.

Chapter 6

The third chakra:

experiencing your
power

The third chakra is located at the solar plexus, just below the bottom of the rib cage. This chakra is where you start to have an understanding of your personal power and ability to have an influence on your surroundings. From here you can take the sensory information of the second chakra of your likes and dislikes and start to plot your own course in life.

This is where you really take ownership of your body and validate your right to create in your own personal way. It is where the ego resides. By allowing yourself to be the way you are and by exploring the paths you choose to take, you can fine-tune your self-knowledge. By understanding what makes you tick you will also gain a clearer understanding of others, and human nature in general.

As spiritual beings we created bodies for one reason: to gain life experiences and refine our understanding of our energy and the universe. When you give yourself permission to follow the roads you need to take in order to gain those experiences, your evolution on an energy level increases greatly. When you focus your attention solidly on your path, you will get there all the quicker.

The third chakra is also where you set the way you run the energy in your body. This chakra helps distribute energy in the right form to the places where you need it.

Trying to control others

The ego can be a very powerful ally when it is focused inward and used for the purpose for which it is intended. When used to validate your perceptions and take action based on who you are, and what you believe, you will find new facets of yourself every day. You will find strength, power and self-confidence through greater self-knowledge. There is a danger, however, that you will use this power and certainty of your will to try to control the will of others.

When you allow your focus to stray outwards, trying to impose your values and beliefs on others, you will quickly lose the insights you have learnt about yourself. It is incredibly powerful to find your own truth. It is foolish, however, to assume that what is true for you is true for everybody.

By way of example, I like my coffee with milk and two sugars. This is perfect for me. It is by no means the only way to prepare coffee. Some people don't like sugar. Some prefer it black. Some people don't even like coffee! There are probably thousands of ways to prepare it. Insisting that people have to drink it with two sugars and milk will probably be met with

ridicule at first and if I were to persist, with increasing amounts
of anger. I may be able to convince some people to do it my
way. Some people may have no preference as to how they have
their coffee. As long as it has caffeine they don't care what else
it has in it! Others may do it because they do not enjoy conflict
and it will get me off their back, but it will usually lead to
resentment in the long run.

In this example it sounds ridiculous, but it happens frequently in day-to-day life. I'm sure most of us know people
who insist on having people do things their way, and we
probably all do it from time to time. When you get into conflict
over the right way to do something you are getting into a grey
area. You can be certain of your own truths, but what is true for
others may be totally different from your views. You can spend
an eternity debating relative merits and drawbacks of different
approaches, but in most cases you end up with an agreement to
disagree. There is enough room on the planet for me to have my
truth and you to have yours. When you let go of having to be
right, and of enforcing your line of reasoning, you will find you
have a great deal more energy for creating your life. Letting go
of these power struggles will give you a greater degree of
freedom and certainty than you could achieve previously.

It may be that one way will work better than another.
When cooperation and sharing of ideas occurs everyone gets to
benefit from the experience of all involved. When one person
seeks to validate his or her experience at the expense of others
and tries to control and manipulate those around, they will
invalidate the experience of others and cheat themselves of a
learning experience. When you try to impose your beliefs on
others, and control their actions, or how they behave, your
energy will be dissipated.

Letting go of what others think you should be doing

We each have our own paths to follow. The more you can follow your own path and discover what is true for you, the greater will be the sense of your power and yourself. This is a continuous process of re-appraisal. A large part of your journey of self-discovery involves letting go of what others believe and working out what is true for you.

Sometimes you will catch yourself behaving like your parents, or reciting words from their mouths. We are usually unaware of what we are doing until we start to pay attention to our behaviour. There may be a large part of your belief structures that you have taken on from others without checking it against what you believe to be true. It is fairly common to have your parents' ideas and thoughts on life ingrained in your subconscious mind. It is useful as you are growing up to follow the examples of your parents, and use their beliefs as a template for yours.

About 50% of our belief structures are in place by the time we are five years old. This is especially so of your mother's energy. She carried you in her womb for nine months after all! That is a lot of time to impress her hopes and fears, her dreams and wishes for you into your subconscious mind. The beliefs of your particular religious affiliation, if you have one, or guru may also be fairly prominent in your belief structure. It is incredible to see how many of our beliefs are on autopilot, and it is worthwhile to take the time to explore this. I am not saying that you should throw away all of this information. It is a great service these people provide by allowing us to benefit from their experience. I am simply saying that you view the information from the perspective of what is true for you. Take what you like from all these sources and let go of the rest.

Setting your will and your energy, and letting others do the same

When you engage in psychic healing you know and experience the real meaning of love. You are totally immersed in it. To a psychic it is simple. When you begin to see the light of spirit within everyone and everything that is, you begin to get the idea that God (love) is all around you. You have something in common with everything and everybody!

For years I just could not understand what 'turn the other cheek' meant. It is so clear now. If someone does say something cruel to you, you can immediately stand back and see where he or she is coming from. Hence now I understand Jesus on the cross announcing to the heavens, 'Forgive them for they know not what they do.' Previously I thought, kill the sods, after totally humiliating me they then put me up here on the cross to die. I hate them all. Well, now I see it differently. My mother, ex-husband, my children and various other people were corded to me in so many different ways I was drained of my energy. Now I have an enormous amount. I cleared them all out of my space. At first it was strange. I thought I would never have anyone to have dinner with ever again. I just did not want to be with anyone who drained me.

A father's or mother's energy is not bad; it is just not your energy. To remain true to your own essence you have to run your own unique energy. No one else's energy works as well for you as your own. You will find energy in your aura from your parents, your friends and family, boss, ex-lovers, people who have passed on from past lives, even your cats or dogs, but none of them works as well for you as your own.

Energy that is not yours has wishes, desires and judgements of others, which are not those of your essence and soul. It clouds your own judgement if someone else's energy is in your space. When you suddenly have uncontrollable emotions, usually it contains a lot of other people's energy. I can distinguish my own energy from my eldest daughter's now. Her emotions used to overpower me to the degree that I though I had 'lost it'. When I sorted out my energy and took it back from my daughter, the effects were amazing. I don't think my protective 'mother' energy enmeshed in her space was doing her any good either, so we are much better off now. We are no longer co-dependent but our own separate unique selves. I respect her soul's journey.

There is a big difference between 'protecting yourself with white light' to shield others' energy from entering your space, as is often taught, and being clear. Being clear is ideal. No one else's energy can stick in your space without your agreement, usually it is unconscious, but it is still an agreement for it to be there. As you become clearer and own your own space, your clarity will protect you.

> Clear foreign energy from your energy field and you will understand unconditional love

Most instances in life are just repeat patterns of the original pain, which may not only go back to this lifetime but lifetimes before. I was a real martyr and chose to be born to my controlling mother and then the experience with my ex-husband. I love all the people that abused and stole from me as it had to get so bad before I could finally see it, acknowledge the pain, release and forgive and move on. Before this, most of us carry on feeling guilty that we 'don't love our mother or father'. When you clear their foreign energy out of your energy field they do not affect you any more and you then can have a healthy relationship without all the energy leaks of controlling, manipulating, limiting and conditional games being played. It is the ego that can get in the way.

Ego

A good way to keep your ego in check and to keep your power working at creating for yourself is to follow the saying 'do unto others as you would have them do unto you'. One thing about this planet that never ceases to amaze me is how there is so much freedom of choice and such an abundance of possibilities, and somehow, everything still works! Rejoice in the freedom that you have to express yourself the way you wish and let others do the same. They will love you for it, and you can learn a great deal if you keep the door open to learning from others. It can only speed you on the path.

Some years ago I visited good friends in New York. Jack was a fabulous guy, good looking and outgoing. He always liked being 'the best'. He was married with three children and wherever they went, it was first class all the way. I loved Jack and his family and I was staying with them for a few days and sensed something was wrong. Jack was in the real estate business and had just purchased another property, in addition to his hotel project which was under way, and all seemed on an upward roll on the surface. But I saw different and asked his wife what was going on, although I knew she did not deal with money and had never even written a cheque. Jack dealt with all that! Of course, she had no idea but I begged her to ask Jack what was their financial position. It seemed they were spending too much money and I could sense it was just not right. Well, Jack was furious that I had dared to talk to his wife and disrupt the family. After all, it certainly was none of my business. Jack was edgy and I said I really was a good friend and if ever he wanted to talk to me he could phone me at any time. I left, but knew I had done all I could have done. It was a red alert area for Jack and he would not let me in to discuss it.

One year later he visited me in spirit form. Then the

telephone rang; it was a family friend of Jack's. Jack had killed himself. He had sent all the children away on a holiday and gassed himself in the garage. His wife was heavily sedated; she totally went to pieces. The bank was coming in the next day to reclaim the house. Poor Jack could not bring himself to tell his wife and family and face the humiliation from friends, so he killed himself. When he appeared in spirit form he was startled to find he didn't have a body and could not go back and comfort his family. He was so down that he was overwhelmed with humiliation and had not thought of how his family would cope. He asked me to help them. He realized that he had been wrong, he had left them bankrupt and the bank was still coming in to claim their house and the children were still at private schools. If only he could have talked to his wife. She was dismayed that he had not felt secure enough to talk to her, and the children were bowled over that their father, who had given them everything and had always been in charge, had kept this biggest secret from them. Everyone was in shock.

This is a prime example of ego. All of Jack's friends raised some money for his family but life for them was never the same again. If only Jack had had the courage to confide in us, we would all have helped him. We all loved him so much. Money and bankruptcy are only things; he paid a very high price with his life. His wife still cries, 'But it didn't matter if we didn't have the house as long as we were all together. We would have worked and sorted it out somehow.' Now she is working and has learnt to manage a family and finances. The children took part-time jobs and continued to go to school. They are a wonderful family.

Meditation for experiencing the third chakra

○ Find a comfortable chair to sit on.

○ Relax and bring your attention to the centre of your head.

○ Get grounded, and get your earth and cosmic energy running (see Chapter 2).

○ Watch your energy running for a minute or two.

○ Bring up a picture of your third chakra on your screen.

○ Notice as many details as you can. What does the chakra look like? What colour is it? What does it feel like? Does it feel strong and vibrant or does it feel heavy and dull? Does it hurt? Is it spinning freely? Do you have thoughts of other people when you focus in?

○ Observe your chakra for a few minutes without judging what you see. Get used to the 'feel' of your third chakra.

○ On your screen out in front of your sixth chakra, put up a gauge for how much of the energy running the third chakra is creating for you. See the information as a number from one to a hundred. Have a look at what other energy is in there and what it is doing. It may be that you are expending a lot of energy in trying to influence what someone else is doing and trying to create for them. You may be trying to resist or process the influence of someone else. Just get a sense of the energy that is focused on your development, and the energy that is distracting you from that.

○ If you wish, you can focus on the energy that is diverting your focus. What messages do you get? Do you get a sense of certain people arguing with you? The more information you get, the clearer you will be as to the issues you are working on and what you need to pay attention to. It is not always necessary to go into such detail though. Many times our bodies are able to release the energy without processing it or reading it any further.

○ Slowly start to turn that gauge up and allow yourself to have 100% of your energy focused on following your own direction. We may make the journey with others, but we should always reserve the right to go in our own direction and break free from the crowd when we need to.

○ Allow the energy to separate, and watch as the distracting energy falls away. Create a grounding cord and let this energy flow down to the centre of the earth. As this happens you may find yourself thinking of people you know, whether it be business associates, spouses or family members. This is an indication that the energy you are moving will change the nature of these relationships slightly. When you change your energy there is usually a period after this when you renegotiate the nature of these relationships, and set new perimeters. Just keep doing what you are doing for the moment.

○ When you have finished, notice the difference between when you started and now. What does it feel like? Did the colour change? Get accustomed to the feel of your chakra with no distractions. Notice every detail, so you will know what your energy feels like, and when your focus is elsewhere.

○ When you are done, fill yourself up with liquid gold energy and open your eyes.

Chapter 7

The fourth chakra:

a calm, neutral space

The fourth chakra is located at the heart, and is also called the heart chakra. It is one of a few places in the body where you can take a break from the decision-making of life and find some refuge for a while. It is a calm and neutral space where you can work on your relationships with others and yourself. In this chakra you take your knowledge of yourself and the information from the lower three chakras and start to really integrate this into your interactions. The first three chakras help you to separate your beliefs and truths from those of others. Here you start to see yourself as part of the whole. From the fourth chakra, you perfect and validate your gifts and uniqueness, and reach out from your body to share this with those around you.

The fourth chakra can also be used as a sanctuary and a place for communicating with the Supreme Being, whatever you choose to call Him/Her. It is where you connect with your spirit, and in turn the God within us all. Your first glimpse of the spirit occurs here as you awaken to the knowledge of yourself as more than just a body.

The fourth chakra is also one of the locations of tension in the body; neck and shoulder problems start in the back of the heart chakra. Diminished kundalini affects the heart, its circulation and breathing. Also the warmth you feel for other people. Denying your heart is denying yourself at the very heart of who you are. When you view from the heart and see people as spirits you have a totally different viewpoint.

Understanding your concept of love

The fourth chakra is best described in terms of love and relationships. Love seems to be one of those words that have very different meanings, depending on who you ask. You can love a bird and keep it in a cage, or you can love it and allow it to be set free. You can even love a bird and want to eat it. There are many different forms of love as well: the love between siblings, the love between lovers, and that between friends. This one word encompasses many different types of energy. In fact, love can be used to describe almost any situation. You have people you love to be with, and those you love to hate. You can love someone and want to do everything for him or her, or you can love someone and give them freedom to do their own thing. Have a look at what the word love means to you. Look at your pictures about what love looks like as well. Try filling in the next sentence:

If you love somebody, you ...?

Do this until you run out of endings for the sentence. Does your version of love mean that you place others before yourself, or does it mean that someone does that for you? Do you feel the need to protect those you love, keeping them close to you, or do you give them space to do what they like? Does it involve spending every minute of the day together, or being able to be independent? Another question you might ask yourself is whether you are prepared to give all of the things you hope to receive from a relationship.

Remember there is no right or wrong answer. When you have a clearer understanding of what love means to you, it is usually easier to create that in a relationship.

One definition of love, which I really enjoy, is very simple but it seems to sum it all up fairly well. A good definition of love is when two people can mutually validate each other. This means that both sides benefit and are uplifted by the experience.

I remember skiing in Lake Tahoe with the family. We had a phone call that my husband's father was very ill and would perhaps die within the next couple of days. We had only been there one day and now we had to return home for him to go to visit his father. My first reaction was one of inconvenience that our ski trip had come to an end so soon. I felt annoyed and I was ashamed that I should feel that way, but I did. I resented having to pack up as the weather was wonderful and we had perfect skiing conditions. I felt so selfish and bad about my feelings that I sat down to meditate and cleared my heart chakra and filled it with unconditional love and compassion. After that I felt totally different. I packed up and comforted my husband; of course we would all go home and get him off on the first flight to England. The resentment had disappeared to be replaced by compassion and understanding.

This state of being is very powerful and I am sure we do not really want to stay in our little world of lower emotions of self-pity, resentment and life is all about me. Being non-judgemental requires that you know your own feelings and opinions, and act on them, while honouring the uniqueness of the other person. Being neutral releases judgement and opens the heart. Our culture has a dichotomy between the heart and the head. When I was thinking with my head all I could think about was that this was terribly inconvenient and why had his father picked this of all times to be ill; we were on holiday! My heart had no such thoughts or opinions, only compassion for a soul about to pass over. I had a chat to him telepathically and said my goodbye, and assured him that his son would be there to see him as soon as possible.

In this day and age, interpretations of love are located in the first four chakras. They can often involve survival, sexuality, power struggles, jealousy, competition, hidden agendas, judgement, pain and punishment. Love can also be an upper chakra experience, which is spiritual. It is in reality, affinity and communication. A touch, a hug, a handshake or a warm body next to yours. Communication is a spirit-to-spirit 'hello' from the centre of one head to another, where the spirit abides most happily and safely. From this vantage point, the emotions of sadness, grief, anger, hate, lone-

> Love is when two people can mutually validate each other

liness and jealously are missing. When you say 'I love you' from a neutral space it means 'hello' as a spirit. There are no hidden agendas, no requirements for you to perform, no commitments. You can love more than ever this way. You can give and accept love on these terms. Expectations and conditional love are the surest ways to kill love that I know. Guilt, manipulation, 'If you loved me you would do such and such', all come into it. Yuck!

For a woman, what does love mean? You own your partner, he is yours? Financial security? Fantastic sex forever? Love is something that fountains freely within your own space to others without limits. This flow occurs without expectations of others. The spiritual body can have this fountain in simplicity and for no effort: it is called affinity. Your heart is awash with love. It is only the physical body that goes crazy in love. Affinity is the flowing, no-effort space that says, 'I see you and you are perfect just the way you are. I can and want to be with you and I am here to talk and share with you.' Together you can create miracles on the physical and spiritual plane and enjoy the game of having bodies that can feel and have sex and love.

But where can love be found? Money can't buy me love, oh no! It isn't cheap and it does not come easy. I always searched for love in the wrong places. Then I discovered I had it all the time and I could only keep love by giving it away. It is blind and selfless and its own reward.

The ability to love

What most of us are looking for is the kind of love that makes us truly happy inside. What kind of love is that? To a psychic you begin to see the light of spirit within everyone and everything that is. But what gets overlooked is the ability to love oneself. If you do not have the ability to love or have an affinity for yourself it is difficult to create love that does not depend on another. This giving away of your affinity for yourself leads to judgement, pain, unhappiness, competition and illness. The lack of affinity for yourself also affects your ability to have or receive. If you hold a negative self-image you will create from the vibration of 'I do not deserve to have this' or 'bad things always happen to me.' Also the feeling that 'the world owes me' sets up. Then there is neediness: 'I need that person to love me, I need that in order to be happy and complete.' This is only temporary and does not solve the problem that something inside needs to be fixed. Tell yourself 'I am complete' and watch how your body reacts.

When I let go of takers, I found I enjoyed my own company more and started to love and nourish myself. When I started to give to myself, guess what happened? Miracles. I gave myself flowers and guess what? My two little sons came home one Sunday with bouquets of flowers for me. I immediately was suspicious, 'What do you want?' They smiled, 'We just want to show you we love you Mummy and appreciate everything you do for us. We want you to do your book and we will do things around the house.' Well, I put the flowers on my desk and inspiration in writing this book came from those flowers and the love and generosity of spirit that emanated from them. They had used all their pocket money to buy them. These little instances mean a great deal to me and my spirit. It is pure simple love, and it makes my heart sing. I feel light and happy that I am loved and cared for. In this simple gesture they gave me their love and energy. A mother runs around all the time giving and doing things for her children, but this makes it all very worthwhile.

The secret to being really happy in love is to love, trust and nurture yourself first and then find another with whom you can share spiritual and physical love. The cleaner the vibration, the more truthful the love and the more satisfaction and happiness shared. The two kinds of love grow stronger and become integrated.

However, it is not always easy to do this and it can take something calamitous in your life to discover why. One day

I had a phone call from a friend in England who had just been told she had a tumour and had to be operated on the very next day. I tuned into her aura and instantly saw a picture of her mother giving her arsenic. Her mother had killed her baby sister when only a one-year-old and she was trying to kill her and her brother as well. I did not want to say it but could not move on until I did. I told her what I saw and she immediately broke into tears. 'Oh, my God, how did you know that? I had forgotten all about it. I was forbidden to talk about it.' She was only five years old at the time and as this was a relatively prominent family in Europe it was covered up. Her father was in the process of divorcing her mother and her mother could not accept the situation. This had happened fifty years ago and her conscious mind had cut it out of her memory. She and her brother were immediately sent to boarding schools and ordered never to speak of this again. It is amazing that the body had held on to this pain for fifty years and it had developed into a tumour.

> The secret to being happy and in love is to love, trust and nurture yourself first

It was a miracle that it was uncovered in the healing. I think it would have taken years of therapy to get to it, if at all. She was a beautiful woman but had always had trouble with trusting in relationships. This was perhaps not surprising once she knew why. She had the operation and cried solidly for weeks. We can successfully block certain things from our consciousness through a process of progressive amnesia, but we expend a great deal of energy suppressing the reality around us. My friend is now happy and healthy and has a wonderful relationship.

Meditation for letting go of the strings attached to love

Once you have looked at your definitions of love and come to a better understanding of how you would like to have your relationships work, you can start to look at other people's definitions of love. What do people mean when they say, 'I love you'?

It is quite interesting to look at a picture of this when someone tells you that they love you. Just notice what you sense. Does loving you entail keeping you in a cage, being possessive and controlling? Does it mean that the person is going to abandon their lives to help you create yours? Does it mean they expect you to drop everything for them? Does their idea of love involve mutual validation or power struggles, and building themselves up at the expense of others?

One big point is whether their love is unconditional or conditional, and what exactly are the conditions. When someone says, 'I love it when you do the dishes. You're so considerate.' Does that mean that when you don't do the dishes you are inconsiderate? Will they love you even if you don't do the dishes?

It is also interesting to see if there are any strings attached to the 'I love you.' When someone says those three magic words, is there an expectation of something in return? You can quickly check this out on an energy level by having a look on your screen.

- ☺ Sit comfortably in a chair. Close your eyes and relax.

- ☺ Get grounded and have your energy running.

- ☺ Create a picture of the person on one side and you on another.

- ☺ See a bubble come from them to you with the words 'I love you' written on it. As it floats over, look at the colour of the bubble, and get a sense of the energy in there. Is it warm and validating, or does it feel uncomfortable?

- ❂ Have a look to see if there are any strings attached to the bubble. Ask each string in turn what it is there for and notice the reply. If it is something you want to keep then you can leave the string there. If not then cut the string.

- ❂ Do this for all the strings in turn. When you are finished. Take the 'I love you' with no strings attached and allow it to go into your heart.

You can also do this in the opposite direction, looking instead at the strings you attach to love, and the conditions you impose. It is fine to have expectations. Most people have them, and most people want something in return for loving you, even if it is simply to be loved back. Being aware of your expectations and those of others will better equip you to decide whether this relationship is right for you or not. It can tell you a lot about how much work may be involved in the relationship as well.

••

Your fiery twin flame

Can't find me love, oh no. Why do we find it so hard? We can go to workshops, work our butts off, have children, slave, give monstrous parties, run multi-billion corporations, run around the world, bend spoons, break glasses, turn water into wine and still be miserable and lonely. Being lonely is good as you learn to love yourself and then the miracle happens. He or she appears. Your twin flame, your soul mate, your true fire-in-the-belly, long-awaited prince or princess.

Do not allow your intellect to misidentify this as romantic delusion. Never stop dreaming and you will find your twin flame. You know him or her as well as you know yourself, you don't know his name or where he lives but with psychic ability his name and where he lives will be given to you. You know he is real, separate but part of you. You know when he is thinking of you and wishing you were with him, you feel his soul's longing for you. You feel yourself increasingly interwoven with him and in need of the warmth of his arms around you and the sound of his voice in your ears, not just in your dreams or in the astral plane, but in your bed and in your life.

Do not let go, you do not have to face death without ever being loved and touched by him or her. That would be the greatest sadness and the biggest waste of all time. You have this wonderful body that wants to meet his wonderful body and enjoy first-to-first chakra great sex and adoration.

Tune into him from your crown, your seventh chakra and your sixth. See the link of golden thread joining you together. Speak to him every day and include this wonderful person in your life. You will bring him in to the physical plane. Believe it, see it, dream it, live and love it. It will happen. Do not settle for less. Most people settle for a pretty dreary and shoddy relationship just for the sake of being in one. You deserve pure love. The love that doesn't care if you are messy, loves you for you, all of you, the sensuous, good, bad and the ugly you. My heart goes out to you and spins warmth in your heart. Let me know when it happens. Bringing in your dream and your fiery twin flame will send ripples out to the universe and give permission and strength to all others to find their own true love. I will certainly celebrate and those in the heavenly realms will celebrate.

I have a perfect example in Julie. She left Asia and flew to London. Julie decided at the last minute to take a side trip to Paris and phoned a friend who immediately invited her to a party. Sam was from Seattle. He was returning to Seattle from Paris that evening and his flight was delayed. He had been invited to a party that evening in Paris but had declined. Now that his flight was delayed he went to the party. Guess who met who at the party? Really Sherlock! You are a genius. Yes, Julie met Sam, they fell in love across a crowded room and that was that. Julie followed her intuition and immediately moved to Seattle. Sam and Julie are marrying this year. What a wonderful tale of love this is. It can happen to you! Just like that, in an instant. Put out to the universe what you truly want and it will come to you.

Write your story and send it to me and I will include it in my next book. If it hasn't happened, take a look at why.

What stops you from having love and abundance?

If you feel a struggle with making your dreams come true, some of your energy may be stuck in past time, or your energy may be so far in the future that you have no energy now. Being in present time is the creation of future time. You only have now and this is where your enthusiasm begins. When you are filled with enthusiasm you have your greatest connection to your higher self or God. It is from this place that you have energy to create and manifest whatever you want to happen. Everything falls into place when a person is ready.

Sometimes a feeling of non-deserving may be at the base of not moving forward. Just being comfortable with the discomfort of a present situation makes it too easy not to change, but the time eventually comes when a change takes place.

We all have a 'havingness' level where we feel comfortable with what we can allow ourselves to have. If you have a small havingness it does not matter how much money comes into your hands. It will disappear until you are left with what you are comfortable with. I have seen multi-millionaires on paper, dressed in a cotton vest, living in hovels. That was their havingness and comfort level. One man in Taiwan was cleaning the floor of his factory. He was worth millions, but was still cleaning the floor. He was stuck, even though he had so much money. So the amount of money you have has nothing to do with your 'havingness' level.

The same is true for career. There may be lessons to play out in your present job before you can move ahead. You will know when the karma has ended, when you are neutral in your response to people around you in the office or at home.

The more you open your heart the more you will open up to the power of the flow and the quicker you will synchronize with the rising vibrations and transform into a higher state of consciousness. If you close your heart and your mind you will be resisting and more of your energy will be spent fighting the very energies that will transform your life and set you free. Your body will get out of sync with the energy around you and your body and emotions will suffer. When you allow yourself to be infused by the high frequency light your body will repair itself and you will not age. You will live in a physical body indefinitely and your mental and psychic powers will know no bounds or limitations.

> You alone
> are in charge of
> your destiny

You are in charge of your destiny and no one else. You can take back your power and take charge of your thinking and your emotions. What you give out, you get back. Your mind and emotions resonate with wavelengths of various frequencies depending on what you are thinking and feeling, also your suppressed thoughts and emotions and attitudes that you would rather not deal with. Anger that you have not dealt with attracts angry people to you. Like attracts like and what you give out you attract. If you think you are a victim of life and blame everything and anyone for your lot in life you will attract and create a victimized, powerless physical experience.

When you exude pure love and believe that good things always happen to you, guess what, they do. When you vibrate pure love, that is what you attract. So if you want love, give it. It is no good blaming other people for your life experiences. You have created them by your own thoughts and feelings. You are responsible for your own life and if you have let others tell you what to do you are still responsible. If you do not like your life and your circumstances you can create new circumstances. Rigid beliefs defend themselves so sternly because the belief becomes the person's sense of self, their sense of security and they would rather cling on to the belief than face the mental and emotional challenge of letting it go. All beliefs are going to crumble. By clearing your mind and energy field of old beliefs and opening up to all possibilities you can be free to tap into infinity. The only way you can learn is from experience and that means experiencing the consequences of your thoughts and actions. If there were no consequences to your actions you could not learn and evolve to higher levels of understanding.

When you open your heart to love, the heart chakra spins with vast speed and power, whipping up the vibration of your consciousness to the highest vibrational expression of life, pure love. As your soul is pure love, you reconnect with the awesome power of your multidimensional self. The vibration of love activates the antennae in your DNA, which reconnects you with the cosmos. An open-heart chakra tunes into the cosmic pulse from the earth and the cosmos, and transmits that changing vibration to your brain and every cell in your body. This transforms your mind, emotions and physical body as they synchronize with the quickening vibrations of this time of change.

We have all experienced the consequences of fear and giving our infinite power to another force be it spouse, boss, parent, teacher, etc. Are you going to leap through the gateway to a whole new state of being? You may have to leave deeply imbalanced people who have disconnected from their levels of self. But you can choose to resonate to the rhythm of love. You only need concern yourself with yourself, not them. It is none of your business what other people think of you. It is not your problem, you can let go of your fear of what other people think and express your own uniqueness. You can stop being a sheep.

You can allow everyone else to do the same and be his or her own unique self. You do not need to impose your beliefs on anyone else; respect their free will and free choice. The only person who knows the best for you is you. That applies to your body as well. As soon as you make an intent such as 'I will have a healthy body', your cells respond. I did that and anything that I put into my body such as food, wine and impure thoughts that was not in alignment with that intent was discharged immediately. You are extremely powerful when you are tuned in and allow things to happen.

The creative force is within us all and wants to express itself. The suppression of this energy leads to frustration, anger and depression. The creative force within you cannot be suppressed and so comes out in imbalanced ways. Hence we have drugs and alcohol to numb and shut off the emotional pain.

By waking up to who you truly are, your life will change, mine certainly did. When you wake up you wonder why you are doing what you are doing. People will tell you that you can't change, you can't do this, and you can't do that. It is limiting and you question, 'Why can't I do that?' Then you take a look at the people who are telling you what you can and can't do and question. Does their life look the way you want yours to be? Is their life even successful? Mostly, it is not, and they just want you to stay where they are. You may have 'friends' who tell you to 'dress down, tone down'. When I go out I want to dress up, when I am at home I want to be comfortable and slob out! Still think you can't do it? Well, you can. You can do anything you like. When fear leaves you will be amazed at what you can do. Your heart becomes awash with love and you are limitless.

My body changed and I look much younger than I did years ago. I look and feel alive and have come out of my prison of dos and don'ts. I am not stiff and rigid any more and playing a role. My mask of perfection covering a body of pain has lifted. I am free to be me at all times. When you open up to the changing cosmic rhythm all hell breaks loose at first. Relationships break up, family and people you thought were your friends walk away. When you focus and ask for what you want in life it will all come to you. You can just be yourself and allow others to be themselves and love them all the same. It is not a time for fear but a time for love, to sing and dance and have fun.

The heart centre or astral body or plane is the realm or level of consciousness that bridges the dimensions of matter and spirit. This is where you travel in sleep. It is the dream world.

Meditation for giving yourself permission to love and be loved

Love is the cornerstone of all our relationships. The heart opens the door to this. Most of us spend our time looking for love outside ourselves thinking that we need someone else to give it to us. When you start to explore and clean up the energy in the fourth chakra you will find that you can connect to an inexhaustible source of love. When you start to romance yourself and fully accept every aspect of your being you will find that you have all the love you need within you. This love is not dependent on anyone else or any external conditions being met. It is abundant and free. Decide that you are worthy of love!

When you fully accept yourself with all your flaws and gifts, you will find that you will start to do the same with others around you. You will find that you naturally give yourself more permission to love, and to be loved. When you recognize and accept your own imperfections, you will tend to be more lenient towards your mistakes and the mistakes of others. Your relationships with others tend to become more genuine and stronger as a result.

The heart space is a very creative space. When you attach love to the pictures of what you want to create, they become very attractive to the people around you. Things seem to fall into place with ease. Focusing on what you love gives you a direction to follow. Surprisingly enough it seems that we make a lot of our decisions through fear. This takes us away from a certain point, but may not always have a clear destination. The more you can make decisions based on what you love, the faster you will achieve your goals.

○ While sitting comfortably, close your eyes and relax.

○ Get grounded and get your energy running.

○ Watch your energy circulate through your body on your screen.

○ Create a miniature version of yourself and go down to the level of the heart. The heart is an area that is designed as a sanctuary. Enter the heart through the front. (I see the entrance as a double door to which only I have the key. Imagine an entrance and go inside.)

○ When you are inside, imagine a large room. Notice all the details you can. See the colour, the feel of it; see if there are any decorations on the wall.

○ Clean up the area and redecorate if you wish. Make sure that it is vibrant and full of enthusiasm. If there is anyone else in there, ask him or her to leave for the moment. You can invite them back again later if you wish, but you do not have to. People can only be here with your permission.

○ In the middle of this room, create a bubble of energy to represent how much you love and accept you. See all the details you can. Notice the colours, look at any pictures and get a sense of what is going on. Look at what is stopping you from loving yourself. Look at any judgements you may have about the subject.

○ Create another bubble to represent you when you totally love and accept yourself. Notice the difference between the two.

○ Attach a grounding cord to the first bubble and allow all of the stuck or old energy to flow down to the centre of the earth. Let the energy from the bubble representing total love and acceptance for yourself flow into the other bubble and replace all of the old energy.

○ When you are finished, allow the clean bubble to expand and fill the room.

○ Sit and bathe in the feeling for a while.

○ Come out of the heart, shutting the door and lock it if you wish.

○ Fill yourself with liquid gold energy and open your eyes.

Meditation for experiencing the fourth chakra

○ Sit down in a comfortable chair and close your eyes and relax.

○ Get grounded and get your energy running.

○ From the centre of the head, watch your energy run for a while, and clean out any obstructions.

○ When it is running smoothly bring up a picture of your fourth chakra on your psychic screen.

○ Notice as many details as you can. What does the chakra look like? What colour is it? What does it feel like? Does it feel strong and vibrant or does it feel heavy and dull? Does it hurt? Is it spinning freely? Do you have thoughts of other people when you focus in?

○ Observe your chakra for a few minutes without judging what you see. Get used to the 'feel' of your fourth chakra.

○ On your screen out in front of your sixth chakra, put up a picture of a scene that represents your relationship with your family. You may choose to separate this into individual members of the family. What is the main theme of the picture? You may see it as a colour that may be vibrant and uplifting, or one that is dull and heavy. You may hear a sentence that sums up that particular relationship, or a few sentences. It may even be a running conversation with the members of your family. You may just get a feeling about it. Get as much information in any way it is presented.

○ Without changing the picture, move it to the left side of your screen for the moment.

○ On the right of the screen, next to the other picture, create a picture that symbolizes your idea of the perfect relationship with your family. If you could have the relationship be any way you wanted it, how would it be? Give it a colour that is vibrant and full of enthusiasm and love. Fill in as many details as you can. Feel how you would like it to feel. Hear the things you would like to say or would like them to say to you. See everybody forgiving each other for any grudges or resentments picked up over the years.

○ When you are satisfied with the picture, compare it to the other one that sums up the relationship now. How is it different?

◉ Attach a grounding cord to the picture on the left of your screen. Allow any old, dull, stuck or angry energy to flow out of the picture and down the grounding cord to the centre of the earth. Allow the energy from the picture of how you would like the relationship to be to flow into the other picture by attaching a cord between the two. Let this energy completely fill the picture as the old energy is flushed out.

◉ If you wish, you can focus on the energy that is leaving the old picture. What messages do you get? Do you get a sense of what it is doing? Are you able to let go of all the stuck energy in the picture? If you sense that there is some energy that does not want to move, try to get a sense of the picture or belief involved. We like to change at our own pace and sometimes we will want to hang on to some parts in order to look at them some more. Just get a sense of it and move on. The more information you get, the clearer you will be as to the issues you are working on and what you need to pay attention to.

◉ When you have finished, notice the difference between when you started and now. What does it feel like? Did the colour change?

◉ When you are done, fill yourself up with liquid gold energy and open your eyes.

◉ Repeat the exercise for a week and see if anything changes. As you do this, do not be discouraged if you clean the picture up and the next day it looks dirty again. It may be that you have reached a new layer of energy. Just clean it up again. Pay attention to your relationship to your family as well during this time and notice if there are any changes.

This method allows the picture to change at its own pace. Instead of attaching a grounding cord to the old picture and draining the energy off it, you can try simply destroying it altogether and replacing it with new one. This is much quicker, but can sometimes be less effective. As mentioned before, it takes time to adjust to new things, and your body feels more comfortable changing a little bit at a time. There are also your other family members who will want time to change their pictures too. This impacts on all of the family.

Another thing that should be mentioned here is that when you create a new picture of any sort, the more it validates all concerned, the easier it will be to create on a physical level. When everyone benefits and comes out better, then creating it is almost effortless. But when you create pictures that invalidate others or try to take advantage of them you will run into conflict and resistance from them.

Search for pictures of being accepted and validated by others

You may like to repeat this exercise with respect to any relationship you would like to fine tune. You might also like to create a picture of you that symbolizes how you see your relationship with the opposite sex, your business associates and your friends or people in general. What is your energy set at when you walk into these relationships for the first time? Are there feelings of confidence or dread? Do you have pictures of being accepted and validated by others or are your expectations those of being misunderstood?

This is a very worthwhile exercise to find out the way that you are creating your relationships. Remember that finding the energy is about 90% of the way to healing it. All that is required for the rest is a bit of amusement and a will to change. It is just a matter of changing the pictures.

Chapter 8

The fifth chakra:

creating your world

The fifth chakra, also called the throat chakra, is where you take the information from the fourth chakra of how you relate to the world and create that in your daily life through your self-expression. How you express yourself, how much you choose to express and how confident you are of your information at this level has a great deal to do with how much you can create in your life. Here you physically express your desires, your likes and dislikes, ask for what you want and set boundaries in relationships.

This is where you take the information from inside of you and share it with the outside world. The fifth chakra is where you communicate your ideas verbally, and on an energy level as well. This is the chakra responsible for telepathy and clairaudience or clear hearing. In this chakra you can talk and listen on an energy level. When you find yourself engaged in conversation with people in your heads, you are using the fifth chakra to process this information. With practice you can develop this extra sense.

The power of speech and self-expression is held in the fifth chakra; the radiance of central truth. If your fifth chakra is blocked, it is very hard to create. If energy is limited as it flows through the throat you have no voice and no projection. In Aboriginal and all other myths, sound and the voice or the word called the earth into being.

In the throat is the etheric body, which is the first in the spiritual realm and is the beginning of one's God-like abilities. The etheric body is the template for the physical body. It is the perfect body, the light body, which underlies the physical body. It is the spiritual matrix for your physical being; a perfect hologram of your life force. The etheric is like your perfect double and your concepts of justice, truth and of perfection itself are all contained within this body or level of consciousness.

I usually see the throat chakra as dark blue and if it is blocked it has a brown sticky molasses substance around it. This is where all your creative energy emanates and travels down your arms to your hands. If is blocked then your creativity does not flow.

Have you ever felt you couldn't say what you really felt? Most of us do and this is where I find most people can't express their true feelings. You must remember that you are not a victim, you are responsible for your own feelings and how you feel about others. Most of us do not want to say how we feel because of fear that we will not be thought of as a 'nice person' and be rejected. This keeps feelings trapped in the throat chakra.

I rarely get sick, but used to suffer from recurring sore throats. When I finally owned my fifth chakra and said what I felt, the release of creativity was tremendous, and guess what? Not only did my sore throats go away, but I found when I told the truth from my heart, without judgement, people respected me more. We all knew where we stood and if we had a misunderstanding it was cleared up immediately.

Most misunderstandings are just poor communication. We do not maliciously go out of our way to harm others without a reason. When you can come from neutrality, playfulness, amusement, forgiveness and acceptance there is no problem at all. I laugh all the time at situations I created, but now I clean them up straight away before my throat gets clogged. I know if I go to talk and it is hard to get the words out, that I have something to clear with someone. If I feel some controlling energy in my throat, I ask myself if I have given away my power to another person, or if I am controlling in some way. If someone is being obnoxious with his or her demands and you do not feel good about it, sit down, meditate and find out why you do not feel good. Resolve the situation by telling the other person what you feel. It may end the relationship, but you do not want relationships that are controlling, do you?

The ability to give to yourself and to value who you are is very important in this world. It is only when you can give yourself permission to follow your path and to be 'selfish' with your time that you will be able to create effectively.

I used to be surrounded by people who wanted me to give to them, to listen and take on their problems and advise them. I noticed it was a one-way street. They were not interested in what was happening in my life, only theirs. I realized that I could not do their work for them, they had to learn their own lessons and these people did not want to change, they only

wanted to dump their problems on me. All for free! I referred
them to other healers, but guess what? They never called them.
They were not really ready to change, things just 'happened' to
them all the time! Drama queens and kings! It was really rather
boring.

It has always struck me as funny that the people
who are calling you selfish are the ones that
want you to give to them all your time and
create for them. Apart from creating on a
physical level, an ability to focus energy on
yourself increases the effectiveness of your
ability to heal others and yourself. It is good
to remember that sometimes when you take
responsibility for the energy and survival of others
you may rob them of experiences they need to go through.

> Give to
> yourself and
> value who
> you are

How much permission do you give yourself to have what you desire?

Here in the fifth chakra you take the second chakra energy of
desire and refine it slightly. You take the emotional charge off it
and express those desires to those around you. When the
chakra is functioning well and the energy is flowing smoothly,
you become neutral to your desires. You are able to express
them easily and without getting caught up in whether you are
worthy to have them or not. When you have judgements about
your desires, then you get stuck. As children, we are at ease
with asking for what we want, but occasionally when we are
growing up we will be scolded or chastised for it. If we get
scolded enough or with sufficient force, then we begin to think
that it is bad to want things or wrong to ask. 'He who asks
doesn't get' is a typical statement. Asking or expressing your

desire is a totally neutral event. The person you express your desire to has a choice whether he or she gives it to you or not.

People will only get offended by what you say because of their pictures and programming and because they are 'stuck'. If you take all of this on you will quickly find that your ability to communicate is severely restricted. People have a choice as to whether they listen to you or not, and they can always get up and leave if they do not like what you are saying.

Always keep focused on what is true for you

This chakra is where you take your personal truths and put them out for the rest of the world to see. It is a certainty that along the line you will encounter people with opposing views, who will seek to invalidate your truths. When this happens you may find yourself taking on their truths – and their criticisms – to see if they have any merit. Your body cannot process foreign energy very effectively. It is like dead space. If you take on this energy, you will know it by the fact that you go over and over what they said and come to a conclusion, only to find yourself going over it again and again. Remember to validate your own information, and when comparing notes it helps to keep focused on what is true for you. There is room on this planet for two people to have different truths on the same subject. We are all each given a body so that we can test our truths for ourselves.

In your meditations you may choose to take a look at how easily you can ask for what you want. See what information you get. Say 'hello' to that aspect of yourself and listen to some of the judgements you may have about expressing your desires. You will find that once you have cleaned this up sufficiently, your ability to create the things you desire for yourself will be greatly enhanced. Sometimes, though, the ability to give to oneself is difficult. We can give to others all the time, just like I did. As hard as it was, I had to learn to be selfish and learn to give to myself.

Selfishness – the ability to give to yourself

Being able to create things is only half the process however. The second part of realizing your desires is to be able to accept things when they are presented to you. It is no good creating opportunities for yourself if you will not allow yourself to have them when they appear, or you do not value your ability to handle those opportunities.

Here is a good time to introduce the concept of 'havingness'. This is simply a measure of how much you can have things in your life. This applies to how much you can have and accept gifts, and it also applies to how much you can have other things like conflict or anger, and still stay neutral to them. It has a lot to do with how much you can accept life on life's terms, with humour and neutrality. As children, our havingness is very high but as we grow we start to form opinions and blocks to having certain situations occur. The subject of havingness is quite extensive, but for now, you can do this exercise.

- ○ Quickly put up a gauge in front of you for how much you can have.

- ○ Turn it up a little every day, cleaning the energy and allowing old energy to flow down a grounding cord to the centre of the earth. Remember acceptance and neutrality are the biggest factors affecting this. Life will happen, and you cannot change what has already happened. Better to accept it and move on.

- ○ Give yourself permission to have things in your life. Treat yourself every once in a while!

Meditation for taking on responsibility

The shoulders and the back of the fifth chakra are where responsibility energy collects in the body. Physically, the expression of 'having the weight of responsibility on my shoulders' or 'carrying the world on my shoulders' is very accurate. Many of the clichés and funny expressions you hear have roots in the world of energy. When you take on the responsibility of creating for other people, your own creations and desires will take a back seat. I talk in more detail about some of the energy games people play to pass on responsibility in a later chapter. Here is a quick meditation you can do in the meantime.

◎ Sit down in a comfortable chair, close your eyes and relax.

◎ Get grounded and get your energy running.

◎ From the centre of the head, watch your energy run for a while and clean out any obstructions.

◎ When it is running smoothly bring up a picture of the back of your fifth chakra and your shoulders on your screen.

◎ 'Light up' any responsibility energy in that area. You can intend that it shows up as little lights or dots or small pictures.

◎ Go through them one by one and say 'hello' to them. Ask it what you are supposed to do and who you are supposed to do it for. Also ask why you are supposed to do it for them. If you decide to let go of it and that you don't need it any more, attach a grounding cord to it and let the energy flow down to the centre of the earth.

◎ Repeat this process until you have finished. It is not necessary to go through all of the pictures, but it is useful for getting more insight into what is going on. If you want to speed things up, simply attach two grounding cords, one to each shoulder blade, and drain all of that out.

◎ Fill the area with liquid gold energy and open your eyes.

It is good to remember that sometimes when you take responsibility for the energy of others you may rob them of experiences they need to go through.

Meditation for experiencing the fifth chakra

The health of your fifth chakra will directly affect the ability you have to speak your truth and to express yourself without reservation. There is so much programming that you pick up about what you can and cannot say, what is polite to talk about and what is rude, and whether you can express emotions like anger or should hold them in. It is common for the fifth chakra to get blocked with this energy, and a good clean on a regular basis is recommended. Practise looking at a picture of the fifth chakra on your screen and 'light up' all of the programming that tells you what you can and cannot express.

- ✪ Sit down in a comfortable chair and close your eyes and relax.

- ✪ Get grounded and get your energy running.

- ✪ From the centre of the head, watch your energy run for a while and clean out any obstructions.

- ✪ When it is running smoothly bring up a picture of your fifth chakra on your screen.

- ✪ Notice as many details as you can. What does the chakra look like? What colour is it? What does it feel like? Does it feel strong and vibrant or does it feel heavy and dull? Does it hurt? Is it spinning freely?

- ✪ Observe your chakra for a few minutes without judging what you see. Get used to the 'feel' of your fifth chakra.

- ✪ On your screen out in front of your sixth chakra, put up a gauge for how much permission you have to express yourself freely, and get your answer as a number between one and one hundred.

❂ Put a grounding cord on the fifth chakra; start to turn that up little by little. Notice what comes up as you do that. Watch as energy starts to leave the chakra, notice how it feels at each level. You may hear tapes of people from your past; old school teachers, parents telling you to calm down or to stop making a fool of yourself. Let all of the energy that wants to leave flow down the grounding cord to the centre of the earth. It may be that you can turn it up to a certain level and then it seems to get sticky or harder to move. If this happens, say 'hello' to the gauge and see what is holding it back. (You may see someone's hands holding the gauge; you may hear a phrase or just get a feeling. Ask the blockage what it is doing there and listen for the answer.) When you have looked at the energy, give yourself permission to move on and to turn up the gauge.

❂ Keep going until you reach 100%.

❂ Bring down a ball of gold energy from the cosmos and allow it to fill the fifth chakra, cleaning out any remaining energy that is stuck.

❂ Bring down some more gold energy. Allow it to fill the rest of your body and your aura.

❂ When you are done, open your eyes and stretch.

Chapter 9

The sixth chakra:

sending and receiving messages

The sixth chakra is made up of a cluster of different energy centres. The two main centres are the pituitary and pineal glands. The pituitary gland controls the functioning of the other glands in the body and is located at the level of the eyebrows. It is an important centre when doing healings. The pineal gland, or 'third eye', is located at about the level of the top of the ears. For simplicity, it is fine to imagine it as a cone of energy emanating from the body at the forehead (see also page 49). Clairvoyance comes mainly from the sixth chakra.

The sixth chakra is where you send and receive images in the form of pictures. This is where you develop your ability to visualize concepts and information. Through this process you can look at how others 'see things' or read their energy. Using the sixth chakra allows you to use your intuition to its fullest potential by taking all the sensations gathered by the other chakras, bringing them together and processing them into meaningful information.

The sixth chakra is also where you can create and manifest by thought although many people fight and resist this. It is the place where I see pictures. One day a potential client came to my office. We sat and discussed her finances. Suddenly her face changed to one of a Roman soldier with a spear, about to spear me. I was startled and excused myself and went to the kitchen we had in the office. I splashed water over my face and cleared my head. When I returned I made sure she looked normal. After five minutes the same vision appeared. Her face literally changed before my very eyes. This was a warning that she was 'out to get me'. I gave her the telephone number of the opposition and told her that we were not what she was looking for, they would do a much better job for her.

Bring together all your sensations and process them into meaningful information

From antiquity, the 'third eye' and psychic sight have been cloaked in mystery. The third eye sees and allows you several kinds of perceptions. It provides you with tools to perceive extrasensorily. It enables you to see what is so, not just what is yours. We tend not to see a complete picture but it is filtered and focused on us as individuals rather than universally. The third eye allows you to see a clearer, more expansive vision. The veil is lifted so you see the real truth. It is the body that holds your future and access to that future. It is the celestial body where the future exists in space and when you die, becomes a star and returns to the divine celestial light from which you have come. This body influences all that light; it enables us to 'see the light'. It is the realm of 'sight' in all of its various manifestations: visualization, clairvoyance, inspiration, knowing, insight, foresight and psychic abilities. Manifestation from thoughts, dreams, fears or any other feelings become reality. The sixth chakra takes man's evolution into the collective and the spiritual as it is aligned with all spirits, living and dead.

Validating intuition

As you use the sixth chakra and get used to consciously running your energy, you will find that the information you receive will become clearer and clearer. You will be able to feel the energy running through your body, hear the answers to the questions you ask, and see the energy flowing through others as well as yourself. Learning to trust and follow your intuition again can be a slow process sometimes. Even those of us who have been running our energy for years have down days where we doubt our intuition. You may notice that when you are with some people you can see very clearly, but with others you have a hard time seeing at all.

One reason for this is that people will communicate energetically using their most developed sense. Some people will send pictures so clearly that you will be able to read all day. Others will only show a few pictures, but they will usually be the most important ones. Still other people will prefer to talk on an energy level or use their emotions to communicate. There is probably nothing wrong with your reading ability. Just gather whatever information you receive, in whatever form it takes, and validate yourself.

Different people have varying amounts of permission to be psychic. Some people will light up when you mention being psychic. Others will either become very disinterested or even hostile. You are probably just picking up on their permission levels for being clairvoyant or talking about energy work. With practice you can gain seniority over this and have your clairvoyance no matter what the situation. The more you practise and get positive results the more you will be able to validate your intuition. Keep at it and you will be rewarded.

Certainty over what you see

Gaining certainty over what you see will allow you to give yourself more freedom to share what you see. Your part in a psychic reading is to simply read and share your impressions. The more you can let go of fears about whether what you are reading is true or accurate, the more you can relax and be at ease with what you see. When you let go of 'trying' to read, and simply read, you will find that your information becomes clearer and more accurate. Your first impression will usually be the most accurate one, because the mind has not had sufficient time to analyse and create a picture of what you 'think' is going on. What you can be sure of in the beginning is that you see what you see. Just give yourself permission to express what you see. With time and practice you will find that you can relax and read without effort and your accuracy will increase.

The more you run your energy and clean up your chakras, the more you will get a sense of what your energy is and what is foreign to you. You will be able to separate out what you read from what people want you to see. When you become aware of your ability to hear and see other people's energy, you will realize that not everything you hear or see is initiated by you. You could be picking up information from others. This information might be giving advice or asking questions. It may be praising or blaming. If you remember to keep your sense of humour and remind yourself of what you are trying to create, you will be able to keep a strong focus.

Forming beliefs and creating your world

The sixth chakra is where you read what is going on and how people have set their energy, and it is also the place where you take your information and create your world through your pictures. Here you create your experience through your beliefs.

There is an old saying that goes 'As you think, so you believe. As you believe, so you act. As you act, so you become.' The pictures you create about who you are, what you can achieve and how others perceive you have a very real effect on your actions. You can also use these pictures to set your energy to create things for yourself and others. When you pray, you are simply setting up a picture of what you want to occur. It is also true that the pictures you have about others will affect the relationship you have with them.

One key element in having your pictures go out and create for you is that you have to let them go at some stage. A lot of religions say that it is better to pray for someone else, and that when you pray for selfish things you will not get them. The reason it works better when we pray for others is that we are able to let go of the picture after we have created it and give it freedom to create. When you create pictures for yourself, you are more likely to hold on to them and to keep pulling them back and updating them. When you get to a stage when you are neutral to your pictures you can finally let them go out to create for you.

The more you clean up your chakras, the more you will understand your energy

When you change a picture, it sends a ripple out across the universe. Everyone you know who relates to you through that picture will have to find a new way to interact with you. When you help others to work on their pictures by doing a healing, the benefits can be incredible.

Being yourself

Here in this chakra you have a chance to focus on what you want and set your energy towards that goal. When you allow yourself total freedom to be the way you want and let go of the mask you put on, you can be more genuine and honest with yourself about what it is you truly want to create. It is by letting go of trying to create these masks that you can free your energy to create the life you truly want.

There is some fear for most people in doing this. The reason you have these masks in the first place is to afford you some safety in the relationships you have. They allow you to fit in to some extent, and to shield yourself from being different. If someone doesn't like your mask, what does it matter? It is not the real you. What happens if you show the real you and then people don't like it?

It is painful when people invalidate your spirit, but in the long run the joy that comes from knowing yourself fully far outweighs any short-term pain. The more you see your true self in all its glory, the more you will validate yourself in spite of what anyone may say.

Meditation for experiencing the sixth chakra

☀ Sit down in a comfortable chair and close your eyes and relax.

☀ Get grounded and get your energy running.

○ From the centre of the head, watch your energy run for a while and clean out any obstructions.

○ When it is running smoothly bring up a picture of your sixth chakra on your screen.

○ Notice as many details as you can. What does the chakra look like? What colour is it? What does it feel like? Does it feel strong and vibrant or does it feel heavy and dull? Does it hurt? Is it spinning freely? Do you have thoughts of other people when you focus in?

○ Observe your chakra for a few minutes without judging what you see. Get used to the 'feel' of it.

○ On your screen out in front of your sixth chakra, put up a gauge for how much permission you have to be clairvoyant, from one to one hundred.

○ Start to turn that up slowly and notice how it feels at different levels. Notice what comes up as you turn it up. Do you find yourself thinking of anyone when you do this? You may start to release a lot of energy which says that what you are doing isn't working, or that it is not real. We call this atheist energy. If you have become aware of it that is a good sign. You have stirred it up and it is on its way out. Just keep turning that up until you reach one hundred.

○ Picture the sixth chakra on your screen, and let any energy that wants to leave 'light up' as little dots in the chakra. Attach a grounding cord to the chakra and allow the dots to flow down to the centre of the earth.

○ Put up a gauge for how much permission you have to be yourself and to create the life you want for yourself. See it as a number between one and a hundred.

○ If you wish, you can turn the gauge all the way down and see what it feels like just for reference, but you do not have to.

○ Turn the gauge up slowly, noticing what happens and what it feels like at each level.

○ Let any energy that wants to leave that chakra flow down the grounding cord to the centre of the earth.

○ Imagine a ball of golden light and see the energy in that ball flow into the sixth chakra, and replace the energy that left.

○ Create a picture that sums up what it would be like if you had the life you always wanted. Fill in all the details you can. What job, if any, would you have? Where would you live? Who would it be with? The main thing is to feel the excitement and energy attached to that picture. How would it feel to have that?

○ Move that picture away from you slightly, and between you and that picture, allow any pictures that are stopping you from having that to appear.

How many pictures are there? What are they saying?

○ Go through these pictures one by one. Attach a grounding cord to each and allow the energy to drain out of them until all of the charge has run out.

○ For each of these pictures that is stopping you, create a new picture that validates your ability to have the perfect life for you. As you create a new picture, allow the old ones to go down the grounding cord to the centre of the earth.

○ When you have finished, notice the difference between when you started and now. What does it feel like? Did the colour change? Do you feel different?

○ When you are done, fill yourself up with liquid gold energy and open your eyes.

This exercise can be split up into shorter segments if you wish. It is quite a lot of energy to move in one sitting and you may prefer to work on a little bit at a time.

Chapter 10

The seventh chakra:

taking
ownership

The seventh chakra is located at the top of the head and is sometimes called the crown chakra. It controls and influences the area of consciousness known as the spirit or the spiritual realm. Your spiritual life, your place of mergence with God, the All, the oneness, is here. This is where you connect with the all that is, and is where you start to slip from time-based reality into the timelessness of eternity. When this chakra is functioning well and the energy is flowing, you find a sense of meaning and purpose to your life. From here you can set the theme of your life and really take ownership of who you are. In order to do this effectively, however, you must allow yourself to let go of the energy games that distract you from yourself. Trying to control others and being in endless competition with people around you will ensure that you will rarely if ever get a moment to stop your energy. These games are very time consuming and require your energy to be somewhere other than where you are now. They will set your energy at 'struggle', which means you will find it hard to relax and find peace.

The crown chakra is the gateway to the other world. A lack of power in the crown contributes to sleep disturbances and prevents states of consciousness from being reached where you connect to your spiritual source.

Connecting to the source

When you connect with the now, you can connect more fully to the vast resources of the universe. You have access to information that is beyond any doubt or questioning. Here you come to intuition that is subtler, but the level of certainty is such that there is no need for you to question it. You just 'know' things.

This is the chakra of prophets and mystics. From here, all of the answers you seek can be revealed in a split second, in the form of revelations or flashes of inspiration. It is where you connect to the Source. Most people believe that you have to 'do' a lot of things in order to find the Source. Meditate in a certain way, chant prayers, follow a certain philosophy. In my experience it is quite the opposite. All you have to do is stop what you are doing, or at least slow down enough to realize that you are always connected, whether you are conscious of it or not. When you stop all your planning for the future, analysing the past and general carrying on, you give your energy a chance to come back into the now, or present time.

Most of us try to use more power and force to achieve things on an energy level when what is needed is for us to use less force and more certainty. We are all incredibly powerful and have infinite potential to create. Once you start to relax and slow things down enough, you will be able to see what is happening with greater clarity and therefore greater certainty.

Meditation for calling back energy – being present

Here is a quick meditation for calling your energy back into the present. Your energy has your own unique frequency and with practice will come back fairly easily. It is useful to call your energy back to you when you work on it, as you can clean up all of it at once. It also allows you to focus on what is happening right here and now. When you have your energy pulled back you can gain valuable information as to where you choose to focus it, and what you are involved in on an energy level.

☻ Make sure you are seated comfortably, and close your eyes.

☻ Get into the space in the centre of your head.

☻ On your psychic screen, watch as you ground to the centre of the earth, and get the earth and cosmic energy running through your body.

☻ Watch the energy run through your body for a while.

☻ Create a bubble out in front of you.

☻ Put a grounding cord on the bubble, and fill it with gold energy from the cosmos.

☻ See a version of yourself, which is just energy, in that bubble, and have the version of you say your full name three or four times. As you do this, imagine all of the energy which is out healing others, stuck at the office, or planning your next holiday coming back from wherever it is and filling that bubble.

☻ As it comes back, ask it what it was doing, or watch the pictures on your screen of the situations the energy was working on. For each picture, decide whether it is something you want to have your energy invested in. If it is not, then allow the picture to flow down the grounding cord to the centre of the earth.

☻ When you have looked at the energy and found out where your attention is focused, let any old or dull-looking energy flow down to the centre of the earth, and allow some fresh gold energy to fill that bubble.

☻ Create a cord from that bubble to the top of your head, and let the energy from the bubble flow into your body and down the channels at the back of the spine.

☻ Let it fill every cell in your body, and when you are done, open your eyes and stretch.

....

Taking responsibility for creating your own reality

This chakra is less about doing and more about becoming. What you do will flow naturally from who you are and what you hope to become. By taking responsibility for your actions and deciding who you want to be, you effectively bring back all of your energy that was previously engaged in blaming and punishing others. It also gives you a great deal of power to change situations. You can change the reality of a situation by changing your mind about how you perceive it.

With your seventh chakra running smoothly you can start to really experience yourself as a spiritual being. Your ability to create is enhanced by the feelings of ease and certainty that come from your connection with your spirit. You begin to make things happen for yourself and start to create and make decisions based on your spiritual path, rather than the more physical needs of the body. When you allow your spirit to set

your energy, you will find that things seem to work out naturally and with ease. More than this they seem to work out better
than you could have planned for yourself.

You start to realize, in a way that is much deeper than mere
thought, that you connect to the entire universe and the span of
your influence stretches out far beyond the limits of your
physical body. You start to realize that as God is in everything,
so you are a part of God. When you realize this truth, you start
to see these qualities in those around you as well. Your relationships and entire life become infused with spiritual meaning
and a sense of purpose.

Meditation for experiencing the seventh chakra

- ❂ Sit down in a comfortable chair and close your eyes and relax.

- ❂ Get grounded and get your energy running.

- ❂ From the centre of the head, watch your energy run for a while and clean out any obstructions.

- ❂ When it is running smoothly bring up a picture of your seventh chakra on your screen. Notice as many details as you can. What does the chakra look like? What colour is it? What does it feel like? Does it feel strong and vibrant or does it feel heavy and dull? Does it hurt? Is it spinning freely? Do you have thoughts of other people when you focus in?

- ❂ Observe your chakra for a few minutes without judging what you see. Get used to the 'feel' of your seventh chakra.

- ❂ On your psychic screen out in front of your sixth chakra, put up a gauge for how much you are in competition with others, and see the answer as a number from one to one hundred.

⊕ Notice all of the people involved, and notice how it feels.

⊕ Turn that gauge up to one hundred to see what it feels like. Stop if it gets uncomfortable for you. Now turn that gauge down slowly, and watch what happens at the different levels. Keep going until the gauge gets to zero.

⊕ Attach a grounding cord to the seventh chakra, and allow any old energy that you are ready to release drain down the cord to the centre of the earth.

⊕ Fill the seventh chakra with gold energy to replace the energy that is left.

⊕ Now put up another gauge to see how much of your energy is set at control. (This can be for controlling others or being controlled.)

⊕ Turn it all the way up to experience what that feels like, then start to turn that gauge down, taking note of how the energy changes as the level goes down. Keep going until the gauge reads zero.

⊕ As you are turning the gauge down, observe any energy that gets lit up and let it flow down the grounding cord.

⊕ Create a bubble out in front of your seventh chakra. Intend that this bubble fill with energy that resonates at a frequency of clarity, bliss and peace. Sense the energy in the bubble. Feel how it feels. Notice the colour of this bubble.

⊕ Allow this bubble to encompass the seventh chakra and start to fill each and every part of it.

⊕ Create a grounding cord and use it like a vacuum cleaner to remove any old energy from the chakra.

⊕ When the chakra is clean and full of this new energy, sit quietly for a while and just observe your energy running.

⊕ Fill yourself up with liquid gold energy and open your eyes.

Chapter 11

Basic
protection
techniques

While exploring the chakras a few ways have been looked at in which you can move energy and clean things up. Running your energy and being grounded on a regular basis are forms of cleansing and protection in themselves. When your energy is running you have a constant supply of fresh energy to help clean any old or stuck energy.

The subjects of cleaning up and changing pictures, which are very effective ways to start healing your beliefs, have also been touched on. Pictures are like filters on a camera. They alter the way you see the world. If you don't like the way the world is there are two things you can do. One is to change everyone else so they fit in with your way of doing things. The other way, which is quicker and infinitely more practical, is to change your pictures and beliefs on the subject.

You can also use grounding cords to drain old energy from your space. This is like taking a vacuum cleaner and cleaning up dirty areas in your house. When you ground any part of your body and start to drain stuck energy from areas of physical pain and discomfort you can get dramatic results. Draining some of the more serious energy surrounding a picture or issue you have will allow you to see more clearly what exactly is going on.

Neutrality as the best protection

The most effective way to protect yourself on an energy level and to clean up any stuck energy is to cultivate neutrality within you. When you adopt a stance of non-judgement in your day-to-day life, there is no need for you to get involved with trying to control, manipulate or fix a situation. You can simply accept a situation for what it is and move on. When you are neutral to others, you can allow them to like you, or dislike you. They can be in cooperation or competition with you. You can follow your conscience, whether it arouses joy or anger in others. If you judge their actions as being 'good' or 'bad', it is more likely that you will fall into reacting to others, rather than acting from your truths and beliefs. If you make decisions as to whether you are 'good' or 'bad' based on how people react to you, you will fast lose your focus and be distracted by trying to please others.

Humour

Humour is one of the best ways to become neutral to a situation. When you can truly laugh at a situation, it is probable that you have already risen above it. You are no longer affected or controlled by the situation. You have worked through the pain. Humour allows you to take the sting out of any energy. It helps to bring the frequency up to a level that is easier to move. When energy is serious, it feels like mud. It is a struggle to work with and you will end up wrestling with it. When you inject humour into the situation, the energy lightens up to the point where it will almost fall out by itself. Cultivating a sense of humour can help those you are working with to relax as well.

Becoming whole again

When you start to get results by running your energy and clearing old issues, you will get a greater sense of your abilities to create miracles in your life. By validating and recognizing these abilities, you will be more self-reliant and will tend to let go of feelings of lack. It is amusing that when you depend on another, your energy is focused on trying to create through that person. This can involve manipulation and control games that take up an incredible amount of energy. With this lost creativity you actually help to make a state where you find it hard to create for yourself. It is a vicious cycle where you lose your creative energy and feel the need to look to others and, by doing this, lose yet more energy.

By pulling your energy back you will quickly find that your ability to create increases at a rapid rate. You will need to clean up some pictures and change some beliefs along the way, but in the long run you will find you have more vigour and vitality. It is usually easier to create something the way you want it when using your energy. If you try to create it through someone else the creation seems to get changed by him or her, if you get it at all. By calling your energy back as described in the chapter on the seventh chakra, you can start the process of becoming whole again. The more you are focused on your own energy, the more you will know what is going on, which is more than half the battle won in keeping your energy running cleanly, and protecting yourself from outside influences.

Cutting cords

Part of becoming whole is to release your energy from the ties that bind you to unhealthy relationships, or ones that create dependency on others. Cords can provide valuable information and insight into your belief structures with regard to relationships. When the nature of the game is revealed and the cord is released, you can update your pictures and protect yourself from the same games in the future.

Forgiving and letting go

When you are involved with relationships that end badly or are invalidating, you can get stuck with feelings of low self-esteem towards yourself, or of anger and bitterness towards the other person. When part of you becomes hurt, you tend to close off that part and withdraw your energy from that area of your life. This is a natural defence mechanism to deal with pain, by setting it aside until you are ready to deal with it.

Eventually you will need to face this pain and clear it, or it will affect the relationships you have after this. When you are stuck on a picture around a particular issue, you will subconsciously end up creating the very situation that led to the pain in the first place.

Say, for example, you have a picture that everyone you care about will leave you eventually. In an attempt to keep these people in your life you may tend to be overly possessive and clinging. This will tend to drive some people away fairly quickly. But just because one relationship ended a certain way does not mean they will all be the same.

If you can let go of this emotional baggage and give yourself permission to be open to different outcomes, you will be able to free yourself from the cycle of creating the same relationships over and over again. Your pictures create for you. Why then would you want to hang on to a picture that says everyone will leave? Better to clean it up and create a new picture that attracts people who want a long-term relationship. The key to doing this is forgiveness.

Forgiving others for treating you in ways that hurt or invalidate you will allow you to move on with your life. It does not mean that you have to be friends with them, or that you forget what happened. It simply means that you stop investing your energy in trying to punish them, or fix them, or making them see the error of their ways. As you forgive, you will become neutral to the event, and as you pull your energy back you will have more energy to create new and validating relationships for yourself.

Another person you probably need to forgive is yourself. By doing this you can let go of taking responsibility for the emotions of others and of beating yourself up for not being perfect. It will allow you to start to separate from the past and to create a new future independent of what came before it.

Roses

The rose is the symbol of love throughout the world. It is given to those we love, to express our feeling for them. It has a natural beauty which shines independently of external factors. It is because of this that it is a very good tool for psychic work, both in clearing and protection. As with all psychic tools, it is a symbol of your intention to heal and what better symbol than something that reminds you to love and nurture yourself and others.

Here are some of the ways in which you can use a rose to cleanse and protect. One protection tool, which is also very good for setting your boundaries, is to put up roses on the edge of your aura and to attach a grounding cord to them. These roses have two important functions. First, they serve to mark what is your space and keep it separate from the energy of others. Second, they can be used to take some of the sting out of energy that has been thrown at you. Just intend that these roses drain the emotional charge from the energy that is being directed at you. In this way you will be able to 'turn down the volume' of the energy and will probably be able to read it better, without the judgement, pain or punishment attached to it.

In your day-to-day meditations create a rose on either side of you and one each at the front and back to collect some of the charged energy that is directed at you. Make sure they are grounded, so that the energy can flow down to the centre of the earth. Some people create hundreds or thousands of roses around the edge of their aura. You can do this if you prefer. Try it out and see which method works best for you.

You can remove old energy from your body by using it to create a rose out in front of you, then attaching a grounding cord to it and letting all of the energy drain down to the centre of the earth. Try intending that all of the confusion energy in your body flows out and creates a huge rose in front of you. It can be 100 feet tall if you wish. Always make sure to fill your body with fresh energy to replace the energy you removed.

You can also use roses like sponges to go through your body and clean up specific energies. These can be used to collect up and de-programme energy while doing healing and readings. Just create a huge golden rose, about ten feet in diameter. Attach a grounding cord to it and give it a job to do. You may intend that all invalidating energy that is ready to leave your body be collected up by this rose. Allow it to pass through your body, from below your feet to above your head, then put it out in front of you and let all of the energy that was collected up drain to the centre of the earth.

Create miniature versions to clean out the chakras. Just create a rose and let it run through the chakra from the back all the way to the front then out of your body. Let it take any tarnish and judgement out of there.

Another way to use a rose is to create one out in front of you, and allow it to resonate with a particular energy, say love, or clarity or enthusiasm. When it is emanating that frequency, allow it to touch your aura and let your aura start to match that energy. This is good for a quick burst of energy. You can also create one big rose in front of you for when you are giving readings and healings. This is really useful for keeping your respective energies separate.

Above all, be creative. I'm sure that with time you will find or create new uses for the roses and create new techniques for healing.

You do not have to use a rose if it does not work for you. Some students prefer to use a laser to blow up energy or to vaporize energy within their bodies.

Chapter 12

Your relationship with others

In this chapter some of the energy dynamics that occur within relationships are explained, focusing especially on some of the methods people use to influence others on an energy level. When you run your energy on a daily basis and become increasingly more aware of yourself, you will become acutely more sensitive and will notice when something has changed.

Whenever you think of someone and focus your attention on him or her, you send energy in their direction. You may be asking a question of them, wanting them to help you with something, or punishing them for not helping you. There are many reasons you will focus your energy on someone else.

Most of the time this focus is temporary, but sometimes you can get caught up in habitual psychic energy games.

Cords form an exchange of energy

When the exchange of energy between two people is long term and constant, it can be seen physically as a cord of energy that runs between the two individuals, usually attached to the respective bodies at one of the chakras.

Cords are usually formed because we believe we lack something and look for that in others. These cords are, in most cases, formed when one of the parties involved is trying to influence the other or wants something from them. They are usually counterproductive to the spiritual growth of both parties. The effect of a cord from someone else is that you are distracted from the path you are on temporarily, and someone else is involved in the process of setting your energy.

When you are sending the cord, you may be able to get someone to do what you want, if they agree to go along with the game for a while. But what it will do is enforce the feeling that you need someone else to do it for you. It creates dependence on someone else and invalidates your ability to create for yourself.

The more you learn to focus on your own path and validate your own abilities to create for yourself, the less you will feel the need to cord others. When you pull all of your energy back to yourself and become whole again, you realize that you are, in fact, complete and you have everything you need within you.

In this way you can detach from others, which by no means indicates that you no longer care for them. When you do not want or need anything from people around you, you are naturally more genuine towards them and you give yourself more freedom to act without hidden agendas. You can appreciate and validate those around you more under those conditions. This usually strengthens relationships. Sometimes, however, you may find that when you let go of the cords that bind you together, you no longer wish to be around some people. You may realize that the only thing that held you together was fear or lack of confidence in yourself. In these cases it is where the friendship may end, but both parties will be able to pursue their respective paths with more freedom. It is a gift for both sides to cut the cords.

As mentioned in the chapter on the first chakra, when we are children we tend to have a cord running from our first chakra to the first chakra of our mothers. This is an agreement on an energy level for our mothers to provide for us, and it makes us feel safe and secure. This type of cord is beneficial, but even here care must be taken to gradually allow the child to grow and become independent. The cord has to be released for this to occur.

Your energy vs the energy of others

How do you know when you have someone else's energy in your space? The more you run your own energy, the easier it will be to tell what is your energy and what is foreign to you. Sometimes when I am giving readings, I will 'space out' and go blank for a moment. This is usually because the person I am reading wants to see how I am reading their energy and, consciously or subconsciously, focuses their attention on the centre of my head in an attempt to see it through my eyes. When this happens, I usually ask the person to say their name a few times to pull their energy back to their bodies and give them a new grounding cord. A feeling of being 'spaced out' or 'fuzzy' can be an indication that someone else's energy is in your space.

If you find yourself 'stuck' going over the same thing again and again, this could be someone's energy as well. It is difficult to process the energy of others through your body, because it is at a different frequency from your own.

Feelings of pressure in different parts of the body, especially on the top of the head, are good signs that someone is trying to 'pressure you into something'. Feelings of pain can also be indications of being corded.

If you are running your own energy frequently and focused on your body you will know what your energy feels like. There is a sense of ease and clarity. You are in the driver's seat. You know which paths to take. When you have foreign energy in your space you will instantly feel different. You lose your clarity and become less certain of the direction you should go. Your ability to focus declines and so does your ability to create.

You have absolute autonomy over what happens in your space

You are the God of your energy. You have absolute autonomy over what happens in your space, so if someone is in there, it is because you want them there or you have made a concession to let them in because you want something in return. You may agree to have someone cord you for a number of different reasons. In some ways it is a validation to be relied upon or looked up to. It is a powerful feeling to have people wanting your help. Your spiritual path and your focus will usually pay the bill for the short-term ego boost though.

Another reason is that you have fallen into sympathy with them. Fixing their problems will give them some short-term relief, but in the end they will have to learn to fend for themselves. From a compassionate stance you can honour them much more by encouraging people to find the strengths within themselves.

Energy games

There are many games that people play on an energy level to hook you in to dealing with their energy for them. Some of them are listed below. This is by no means a complete list, but it will show some of the dynamics of these games. Some games are designed to actively try to control you. Some are more passive in nature. Some are obvious and some are much subtler.

Any time someone can get you out of a neutral state, they will have a better chance of being able to programme you with their agendas. As always, a sense of humour and non-judgement is the best defence in all these situations.

The sympathy game

Come down in the mud with me. Have compassion but do not join them to heal them. If you do not play their game maybe they will come up to you. Stuck energy in your space is not yours, put it in a rose and explode it. Move energy out with your mind. Don't let people suck you in. Watch your part though. If you solve their problems for them they will do it again and hate you for solving the puzzle. 'You idiot, now I have to do it all over again.'

I remember my daughter after I had rescued her from drugs and their consequences for the umpteenth time. We were sitting at the table and a voice boomed out, 'Will you stop rescuing me, do I have to die and be born again to get this addiction lesson!' I was totally shocked as I thought I was doing the right thing by helping her. No I was not. The moral is, if anyone wants help, let him or her ask for it and really want it. She had asked me many times, but obviously her soul was not ready.

'You have to save me!' Feel the heat without going through the pain and getting burnt. Get luke warm and regard it as a life experience. It has not been in vain but create the lessons without getting burnt.

No one can save you, only you. Find your own truth. Do not base your truth on my experiences. Do not make someone else a guru. You can go to the same astral plane as anyone.

The poverty game

If you have nurtured your mind and body but not your spirit, your spirit may take your money away. Spirit sees money as a threat if you are putting all your time and energy into making it and spirit wants nutrition and evolution. You can have money and be spiritual. Just make an agreement with your spirit. 'Okay, I will spend five days making money and two days we will go to a movie, play and have fun. Is that okay?' Spirit might negotiate for four days of fun but there we are. That's the breaks.

Make spirit your friend and make mind your friend. If you tell your spirit lies or make an agreement and then disregard it, it will hit you with a Mac truck.

Stay in neutral, right from the seventh chakra to the third. Say, 'I am a beautiful, talented, intelligent and powerful man/woman.' Come home to your body. Pull your energy out of other people's space. This will allow their creativity and yours to grow.

The competition game

I know we are all taught and encouraged to compete, but let's see what competition does. I have received many love letters of thanks from friends and people who have read my books and had readings and healings from me. 'Carmel, you are the most wonderful person. I have gained my freedom, my health and love for my family.' I have a cabinet filled with these kinds of letters from sensitive people. They found inconsistencies in their relationship with families and friends on what was called love. Conditional love seemed to rule. 'If you really love me, you will do this. If you love me, you will do that. If you really love me why can't you save me?'

Competition is the bad word here. Competition is the worst destroyer of spirit. Competition takes over your inner space so much that you mimic other people's mannerisms; think and talk like they do. Did you ever say to yourself that you would never be like your mother or father, only to find yourself years later repeating and acting the same way they did? You seem to have no control over your own self.

When someone is competing for you to be the most important person of his or her life, the person most harmed is the one who is the most sensitive. Brothers and sisters, mothers, fathers, mothers-in-law or your very own children may be in competition.

They all know more about you and how you should act than you do. This carries on until one day you let out a big scream and run for the hills. I screamed at fifteen and ran for it.

I screamed after fifteen years with my first husband when one day he invalidated me once too often. He tried to strangle me. His fingers squeezed my throat and I thought I would certainly die. My spirit left my body and I could see my young daughter beating him and forcing him off me. I did not want to go back into my body but wondered who would look after my two children. Reluctantly I returned.

The next day he started calling me names and I felt a red rage come from my first chakra. It was so intense it carried up through my body and I grabbed a wine bottle on the table. He was a 6 ft 2 in big policeman and I had always been afraid of him. This red rage certainly wasn't. I started to hit him and hit him over the head. He cowed and cried out. When about to deliver the last blow, a voice said, 'If you strike him again you will kill him.' I hesitated in mid-stream and dropped the bottle like a red-hot brick. I was shaking uncontrollably. 'Get out before I kill you,' I screamed. He was so shocked that he did crawl out. Fortunately, all his drinking buddies did not believe I had beaten him up. Not a sweet gentle little flower like me!

The lesson I learnt was to follow my heart and inner strength and not listen to what others told me about myself. You are the only person who knows what you can do, and when you can validate yourself you don't need anyone else to validate or approve of you. You do not need to compete any more. You can forgive.

Forgiveness

Sometimes, it is not all it seems. What an amazing boost when you discover you too can release this energy in others. You would think I would still be furious at my first husband who drove me to such extremes, but I am not. I was able to forgive him.

I was looking through my readings recently and I found one I had some years ago. In the reading I was told, 'Before you were born you were with a spirit who in this lifetime you will hate. He is saying to you, "In this lifetime you will hate me my dear, but I am doing this because I love you so very much."' As I read this, tears stung my eyes and I really grasped that it was true. Now I understood what was meant.

I had been married to my first husband for fifteen years and his drinking was truly a test of strength as I had to deal with his continuous emotional outbursts and erratic Dr Jekyll and Mr Hyde behaviour. His emotional body was being destroyed from his continuous drinking and his antics at times seemed very cruel. It is very hard when your loved ones destroy themselves under your very nose and you can't do anything about it.

He eventually died of alcoholic poisoning. It was quite strange because I had just been scuba diving in Fiji with some wonderful friends in their amazing luxury yacht. We were totally pampered and spoilt. After diving I was very relaxed and happy and went to Hong Kong. I was in the Mandarin Hotel and I woke up at 4am to see my ex-husband sitting on the end of my bed. I wasn't afraid though. I just said, 'You have died, haven't you?' He nodded his head and said, 'Yes I came to say goodbye. Please look after the children. I am sorry for what I did to you.' He disappeared and I phoned England where he was living with his new girl-friend. 'Yes,' she confirmed, 'he just died. How did you know?'

Forgive and you will regain all that lost energy

I was able to place notices in the newspaper and inform police headquarters in Hong Kong and I went to his favourite club for a drink with his friends. The same people were sitting on the same barstools after all this time. They cheered when I walked in and I said, 'Let's have a round of drinks for him, he would like it this way. But you can buy, he spent so much money in this club.' That is how we gave him a send off.

This gesture enabled me to pull all my energy back from those years. I also went to the church we were married in and sat down and saw our marriage with all the hopes and desires I had of a young girl in love. My eyes bright with anticipation, not knowing what was ahead. Like a lamb to the slaughter I walked down the aisle. My mother had warned me and while I was dressing she put a hole in my wedding dress from her cigarette. Maybe that was a warning that I did not listen to.

When using psychic abilities as spirits after learning that

you are a spirit, you start to see the competition energy that gets stuck inside you. You discover that a negative energy has been put over you like a blanket, over you and your mental capabilities, and you can't perform, especially around those people who are trying to own you. My smallest son says the other person's voices get in his head and he can't think straight or do anything right.

The 'poor me'/saviour game

The 'poor me' game is an attempt to gain energy from others by getting their sympathy. There are many variations to this game, and many different payoffs. The natural complement of the 'poor me' person is the saviour. On a physical level, the victim feigns helplessness and the saviour comes to the rescue.

The payoffs for the victim are that they have roped someone else into doing their work for them and taking on their responsibilities. On the other hand, loss of self-esteem and feelings of powerlessness are common. The saviour gets to be validated for saving the day and for being selfless. This energy could be used for creating for himself.

There is a similar game on an energy level where the victim will put him or herself down. The saviour has another wonderful opportunity to step in and help lift the spirits of the ailing person. The compliments from the saviour are pleasant and uplifting, but when you make someone else responsible for your emotional stability then you will probably get hurt eventually.

'I have more problems than you do' competition, sets the scene. They manipulate you to steal your energy. They continually 'up' you. 'I have a much bigger problem than you do.' 'You should feel guilty and feel sorry for me.' This starts in childhood. In Australia, much of the time and energy spent on my education went into teaching me the importance of being sorry. 'Say you're sorry!' 'Why, what did I do wrong?' 'You'd better apologize or else!' 'Sorry, what did I do wrong?' Eyes went to the ceiling and a gasp of exasperated air escaped the mouth. 'And what do we say now? You're sorry.' Sorry for being alive? An adult stepped on my foot and I shouted, 'Get off my damn foot!' I immediately got a clip around the ear. 'What did I do? He was on my foot!' 'Say, I'm sorry to bother you, you misplaced your foot and it is on mine. Would you please remove it, if it is not too much trouble.'

Many people are intoxicated on serious energy and phobias. You can raise your vibrations from grey serious, which is low and thick and full of pain, to amusement, which is light and painless. If anyone makes you feel guilty, you can't have this much fun, it is a lie in your space. Your spirit cannot dance its dance in your body until it is cleaned up. You can be a cheap drunk when you are released. They don't have anything over you. By owning your own space, set at safe and comfortable and stating, 'I am not in agreement to being depressed,' you are free.

It is important not to go into sympathy to the extent of absorbing the other's illness. By being neutral and by grounding you can accomplish this.

When I went into sympathy with my eldest daughter my energy leaked away. I was mentally and physically drained but did not know how to disconnect. I realized that after I agreed with her, 'Oh poor you, what can I do to help?', when I was physically and emotionally drained from running around fixing everything, she immediately attacked me. Look at you, what use are you. You used to be so full of energy now what use are you? Help me, huh? I had competed with her 'poor me' syndrome and she did not like it. It is better to remain in a strong position and not take on competing with the 'poor me's'. You will never win and it isn't fun at all.

When my daughter left home my youngest son remarked, 'I saw her boyfriend today and he looks just like you used to look.' 'What do you mean?' I said. He laughed. 'You know, that run down sad hopeless look like you can't do anything to help or change the situation.' 'Yes,' I giggled. 'I am lucky not to be trapped in that any more.' How did I get out of the trap?

When people are being obnoxious, angry, sulking, or withdrawn, these are ways to steal your energy or the energy of others. When you focus on them your energy is going to them. It is like rewarding someone for being bad. Much better to withdraw your attention and focus on positive things going on in your life. Whilst you are wasting your time and energy on the negative it blocks off the positive. Let go of trying to work out why they behave like that. When you take a step back and see that these people play the game with everyone, it would not matter if it were you or someone else standing there, it is easier to become detached from these games.

Is it your responsibility to fix these people? I don't think so. They will learn their lessons eventually, as will all of us. Why would you need to punish these people when they are punishing themselves by living at that energy level? If you get pulled into the attack and defence, you will be playing the same game and you will be at their level.

The victim game

This is a great place because everyone has done everything to you. You have done nothing wrong. It is everyone else's fault! Guess what? Being a victim you have no power. You have given it all away and in your ultimate state of creativity you have allowed people to take advantage of you to play this game.

There are some rewards: sympathy, poor me, a twisted sense of being a martyr, freedom from blame. But look at what you have lost: dignity, self-respect, confidence, power.

In such a situation a victim can do nothing to change his or her circumstances until they take responsibility for their lives and what they allow to happen to them; who they choose to spend their time with and how much power they give to others. It is really an invalidation of the spirit. God did not want his favourite people to go hungry or to suffer through life and it is not spiritual to be a whipping post for others to let them run their pain and punishment through you.

The anger game

Anger is often used to make people think they are wrong and is used to confuse you so they can get their own way. It is a game that says, 'I will punish you unless you do what I want.' Most people are afraid of confrontation and anger and want harmony in their lives so will do anything to keep the peace. In the short term you may get what you want but in the long term you will push even the most compassionate people away.

Anger is a tool for moving people out of your space who you feel are encroaching upon it, but it is a very destructive energy. If used habitually you get loneliness and separation, despair and a feeling that no one listens to you any more because everyone has stopped caring. Again, take a step back and realize that most people get angry then look for others to dump it on. Can you allow someone to get angry without taking it on and trying to calm that person? When you are around someone that is angry are you affected by it? Do you acknowledge their anger as being their own and not any fault of yours? If you take a step back you will realize that most people get angry then look for others to dump it on. Either that or you didn't do what they wanted you to do.

A bully uses anger and intimidation. They are very powerless people who need to push to get things their way. They would not do it unless it worked to keep you on your toes and afraid of them.

The fear game

Fear is the only thing that keeps you from being a happy and wonderful person. Often companies use fear as a way to keep employees in their place. The employees are afraid of losing their jobs and their salaries, so march to the tune of the drummer. They will do whatever it takes to keep the job, at great cost to their spirit. It is a genuine fear and I experienced it when I stayed in my first marriage for fifteen years. I was afraid to leave. The greatest irony was that I was afraid to strike out on my own with two children to support. I did not have confidence in myself. I was afraid I would not be able to earn a living. I even thought about his pension if he died. However, it was all just fear. When I did strike out on my own, my one month's salary soon amounted to more than my ex-husband made in a year. When I had my financial company I made more than his pension and all he had earned in his lifetime. Fear gets in the way and it is mostly unfounded. I just could not see it under the cloud of confusion that was created in the house. He created it so I could not see it, I could not see my strength because he invalidated me every day and I believed him. After I meditated and came into my own energy field I became strong and realized it was all a lie. A lie to keep me with him to take care of him. I was the slave and he was the master!

> Fear is the only thing that keeps you from being a happy and wonderful person

Bosses in charge of major companies keep themselves separate from employees by using fear to intimidate. It works, but creativity cannot flow in those circumstances. It cuts out all creativity as the fear blocks the flow of spontaneity and creative efforts. Employees are just too scared to voice their opinion or new ideas.

Fear permeated the bank where I worked for two years. Senior executives used to cringe at the thought of going to see the manager because if they had done something wrong they would be under threat of being transferred to an undesirable post. When I left I went on to receive three times the salary in a young creative firm and I loved the challenging work.

Schools use fear too to intimidate pupils into following all the rules. I never use fear and my children are free to say whatever they feel. They are amazing in what they observe and have valid and useful information.

The honesty game

Deception requires excuses and always leads to a weakening of a moral position. Even if the deception is successful, you will always have to use energy to protect that and hide the truth, thus wasting energy. The only deception that works is the deception you plan yourself! Built on the premise that there is something in yourself that you are ashamed of or out of harmony with, what you know is right has the effect of blocking yourself off from yourself because you have to ignore what you know is right. Ignorance cuts you off from your spirit. It is not hard to get a sense of spirit. To merge with and live with spirit is more difficult because you have to give up the games that are rooted in fear and separation and be honest with yourself and others. Then you can do what you know is right. Bring your body into integrity, integrate and merge with spirit, merge with your beliefs, your truth and what you believe is right. Honesty is the best policy.

The blame game

One very interesting game is the blame game. If we can blame someone else for a situation, and can get him or her to take responsibility for it, then fixing the situation is not our problem any more. It is usually the case that all parties concerned help create the situation. On an energy level, there is an agreement on both sides to create a situation, so it is everyone's responsibility.

The guilt trip game

When we can make others feel guilty for their actions they can be manipulated very easily. This game preys on the good nature of those people who are usually close to us. People will feign hurt feelings and hope you feel remorse for subjecting them to emotional turmoil. If this happens, then you are more likely to do things their way in order to fix things up.

The 'you didn't do good enough' game

This game is one that healers in particular should watch out for. This is a game where people will tell you that you didn't do enough, or as well as someone else, or that you could have done better. If you buy into this game, you will probably end up healing them 24 hours a day. It is hard to please these people some times. Validate what you do and try to leave the comparisons behind.

Non-attachment

Once you are personally empowered, you can interact in every situation, contributing the highest degree of insight and wisdom without needing to control the outcome of events.

You might work in an impersonal fear-based office and then go home to a dull and faded house. Where does your soul get uplifted and play? In the subway or bus on the way home with all the other miserable people? Be careful not to take the grey serious energy home from the office or allow your spouse or significant other to bring it home. You may be exchanging energy and allowing the grey serious energy to dominate your household.

In readings I have noticed that the brighter people are, the smaller their problems. I stay neutral and speak the truth of what I see and what their spirit wants to communicate to them. I look over hedges to communicate with their spirit and not at the façade of their pain and problems or the mask of perfection that they mostly try to project.

I know that in the money business I projected a mask of perfection. Successful, dressed up in stockbroker garb, trying to look like I was going somewhere. In fact, I was all dressed up and going nowhere, but on no account was anyone else to see that, it was well hidden. It was only when a male client said I looked like a police lady that I changed into designer chic. A Chanel handbag replaced my briefcase and I found I could look feminine and still be successful.

Underneath the mask of perfection, my spirit was withering and wanting out. In fact, after a few years of the money business, when I was talking to clients about their portfolio, I was very tired. When I was talking about energy and healing, my spirit came back into my body and my energy shot way up. I spent an hour with most of my clients and fifty-five minutes were on them and five were on their portfolio. They always left a generous sum for me to invest for them though and I realized that they were actually coming to see me for a healing. They felt better about themselves when they left and we talked about their personal problems and what was going on in their lives. It was then that I realized that energy was more important than money. The light bulb came on! Money is energy too, but we leak out our personal energy a great deal to get money. Some clients were actually abusive but as they were clients and I needed them (or so I thought), I let it slide. I was the golden girl and it was all their idea if they made money in the stock markets. If they lost money I was 'that bitch'. I was selling my soul and my soul did not like it one bit. It wanted to play.

Spirit had said I should give up the financial business and write books and do energy work. I swiftly replied that I was very happy doing this thank you very much and they could find some other donkey to write books. I was Ms Success, making masses of money and was enjoying it. Spirit said that I had agreed to do this work before I was born. Oh, a likely story. Pull the other one. Well Spirit has a way of getting its way. One day everything collapsed. Ten very good clients took out their money from my company. The Securities Commission phoned and said a client had reported me for mishandling her money and they wanted all of my records.

That night I dreamed that my son was blue and had a drug overdose and saw the ambulance. I phoned Australia and my daughter said that everything was okay. I could not get it out of my mind. My father who had passed on came through to me telepathically and said that it was true. My son was injecting heroin and I had better go to Australia straight away. He added with a wink that I would have to take my sense of humour with me as I would certainly need it. He was right. On arriving in Sydney I found that my son had spent the $25,000 that I had given him for university tuition, etc., on drugs. My whole world as I knew it was collapsing and I fell to my knees. 'Why is this happening to me God? Why do I deserve all this?' I heard a chuckle from the heavens and a flash went off in my head. 'Oh, remember your agreement. Well you can go kicking and screaming or you can go peacefully and willingly, but you will go.'

There was no way out, I was trapped into submission. It was a fight with God or my soul but I clearly saw the options. My life in Hong Kong had come to an end. I could carry on and fight the Securities Commission, but of greater importance and dearer to my heart was the possibility of my son dying of heroin. Writing books and doing this healing work suddenly seemed very appealing and I instantly agreed to do it. 'Okay you win, whatever you want me to do I will do it. Clear away all this pain and punishment from me.'

> Let go of judgement and clear your fears and you will become neutral

Well, if I did not believe in energy and a higher power then I certainly do now. At 9am, the Securities Commission called and said the client had withdrawn the complaint. They had checked all my company's books and all was in order. The clients who had withdrawn their money all phoned and said they did not know exactly why they had taken their money out, they had made a great deal of profit and were very pleased with my performance. They would like to invest again. This was a test right in my face and I said that I was moving out of the financial business and would be developing my writing. My whole body withered in pain and agony at all that money I had said no to, but I knew in my heart that it was the correct thing to do.

Moving to California was a whole new experience in energy and clearing my own personal issues. To evolve, it was time to clear them and I now know it was the only way to do this work. To be totally neutral and non-judgemental, you have to clear your own fears and pain out of your body, you have to let go of judgement.

Letting go of judgement

In letting go of my own judgement and doing readings I saw how negative judgements affect a person's self-love and ability to create. If you have an opinion or a concept of something that you see in another person that you do not like, check within yourself to find the matching belief. If you resist the energy that you are looking at in another person in the form of negative judgement, you will create more energy added to your preconceived judgement. What you resist persists. It is like glue, which will stick these judgements to you.

Self-judgement can make you feel that you are not good enough, you are not doing it right or you do not look good enough. These are all concepts of perfection and can basically be detrimental to having, validating yourself and taking action. You go against yourself when you hold negative judgements about yourself. This is what all the advertising hooks into to make you buy their products. If you hold a negative self-image about yourself you will be mesmerized into the images presented on the television of how you think you want to be.

If you find that you have these considerations around judgement, forgive yourself and find some humour in it and then you will detach from it. A way to work on this is to visualize a grounding cord from the base of your spine to the centre of the earth and get yourself centred. Take a couple of deep breaths, allow all the energy of judgement out of your body, releasing it into a big bubble out in front of you. When you feel complete, allow yourself to visualize a golden sun with bright light above your head and draw it into the body, filling in the places where you previously released judgement.

When you learn not to judge others and totally accept them, not wanting to change them, you can simultaneously learn to accept yourself. This is so freeing I can't tell you. It frees up so much energy. When I finally accepted myself I had a good long belly laugh. I had taken my work and myself so seriously. To fit in with the plastic people and society I had bought so many clothes and products and developed the migraine-like squint, which seemed to be the only way to get in the social pages. It was perfect. It accentuated the crow's feet around the eyes and the squint-like eyes enabled me to walk around the cocktail circuit and not see anything, while warning other socialites to stay away from me.

All the clothes had developed into clutter around me. When I tried on all those suits with shoulder pads they looked like someone else. My girlfriends and I went through my closets and laughed and laughed. Who was that person? Was it anyone that I wanted to know? Yes, she was a girl from the gold fields just trying to prove that she was 'good enough', she could have all the money she wanted to buy what she wanted to look good to get approval from others that she was okay. You see she needed that when she wasn't giving herself validation and self-approval. Other people's opinions go into your body like cords and have a damaging effect on you. When you have your own self-approval that you are good enough, no one or nothing can invalidate you or bring you down. You can just detach and look at them and say, 'They are running judgement energy. What are they trying to project on to me? That is their issue and they can have it.' Or it may, in fact, be valid where you can look at it and thank them. 'Oh, I can take a look at this. Thank you for sharing.'

Release invalidation and you will start to reclaim yourself

When travelling to other countries I observed that parents believed that children could be born with special talents or aptitudes. Imbued with the spirit of fairness, Australians believed that all children were born the same and must actively be discouraged from becoming in any way different, better or more capable than their peers. No one could understand why I had a competitive spirit. Why would our normal family bring forth a child who wanted to succeed in life for no explainable reason? The affliction had struck at random. The golden treacle rule in rearing children was, 'You had better not teach them too much as that might give them an unfair advantage over others.'

> When you have your own self-approval no one can invalidate you

There were a series of 'don'ts' uttered clearly and with dramatic authority from early infancy. Instead of, 'You are so cute, I love you,' I think I heard the word 'don't'. The purpose was to impose a feeling of guilt for every action, never or rarely explaining what I had done wrong. If I were to say, 'You look upset,' my mother would reply, 'No I don't.' 'What did I do wrong?' 'Forget it.' 'I want to know.' 'It doesn't matter.' This dialogue kept going until I gave up. It seemed I lived in a house of fear and that I had done something terribly wrong, and there was something bad and wrong about me. I was basically a rotten egg. I crept around on eggshells most of my childhood, hoping never to be spotted, found out or accused. A bit like the Pink Panther.

The invalidation I had as a child stayed with me and lodged in my first, second, and third chakras. All the emotions churned in my stomach and I always felt I just could not stomach this any more. It was not until many years later that I released this toxic energy, like bile from my system. It had kept me back and limited me a great deal. It was quite a rebirth to release it. And it was the start of owning my own body and reclaiming me, the start of who I was, not my mother.

Watch your speech. It is telling you what is actually happening to you. When you say, 'He is a pain in the neck,' you can actually feel a physical sensation in your neck and 'he' is cording you. The list is endless. I'm sure you can think of other games to add, but you get the general idea.

Meditation for cutting cords

Now you have looked at how cords are formed and some of the games that allow these cords to flourish, you are ready to learn how to remove these cords.

- ☸ Sit down in a comfortable chair and close your eyes and relax.

- ☸ Get grounded and get your energy running.

- ☸ From the centre of the head, watch your energy run for a while and clean out any obstructions.

- ☸ When it is running smoothly bring up a picture of your body and aura on your psychic screen.

- ☸ Observe your aura for a few minutes without judging what you see.

- ☸ On your screen out in front of your sixth chakra, change the channel and intend that all of the cords coming into your first chakra that you are ready to let go of light up. If you don't see any cords at all, congratulate yourself and move on to the second chakra.

- ☸ If you do see any cords, gently give them a tug, and see who is on the other end of them.

- ☸ Work on one cord at a time. Ask the people involved what the game is and what agreements are keeping that cord in place. When you have read the information about the cord and decided to let go of it, gently cut that cord where it meets the body with a pair of psychic scissors, or a knife if you wish, and push it outside the aura.

○ Fill any holes, gaps or rips in the aura with fresh gold energy, and attach a grounding cord to the chakra. Allow any energy from the person involved to flow down the grounding cord, along with any pictures about the situation.

○ Repeat the process until you have looked at all of the cords in that chakra, then move up to the next one, until you have done them all.

○ When you have finished, notice the difference between when you started and now. What does it feel like? Did the colour change? Do you feel clearer?

○ When you are done, fill yourself up with liquid gold energy and open your eyes.

It may take a while to complete this meditation and it may be that you wish to divide it up into more manageable sections. You can do one chakra at a time if you like. It may be that one or two cords are all you will want to do at one time, and this is fine also. Listen to your own body and its desire to go at its own pace.

Conclusion

After I learnt psychic healing I found I was not getting caught up in taking responsibility for people and not taking care of them any more. My martyr pattern dropped away when I realized this was not serving anyone, especially me. I used to take people's tales of woe into my body and try to solve all their problems to make them feel okay about themselves. People who cannot match my vibration are now draining away. No longer am I listening to their problems and doing their work for them, they have to do it for themselves. They can have a healing if they are really ready to change.

Now there is nothing stopping me from my path and no one can pull one over on me. This is freedom to create what I want for myself and live a full and happy life.

If you are stuck on anything and can't seem to move on, I hope that you will benefit from applying the exercises and meditations in this book. Remember that if you are not prepared to make an effort, things and people in your life will remain the same. This is no dress rehearsal; why not make the most of your life this time around?

Giving you back to yourself is the greatest gift you can give and the techniques outlined in this book will do just this. You will become a pure, unique and loving individual who holds no guilt, judgement or worries, who is free and full of love and joy for each adventure in life.

I have enjoyed sharing my life with you and hope you can resonate to it and maybe redirect your energies to a better place for you. Remember there are no mistakes with spirit. What may look like the end of the world to the conformed social scene, school and workplace, really may be your spirit having a ball. Don't ever be hard on yourself, laugh and have fun!

Christopher and I wish you all the very best and hope you will enjoy your journey in reaching for the stars! Wave to us on the way and blow us a kiss.

Receiving
and giving
healings

When you are ready for a healing, the healer will appear. When a person asks for a healing, I ask them to say their name three times, then send their mother and father home and take out all judgement energy. I see their whole blueprint of their lives, past and future. They must always ask, as it is invasive to tune in and see without their permission.

When beginning a healing you scan the client's body with your hands to obtain information about blocks in energy flow, damaged chakras, etc. Feel the edges of the recipient's aura by holding a hand above the body and moving your hand until there is a sense of contact or presence. This feels like a slight pushing sensation against your hand. Move your hand along the aura from feet to head and as you move your hand sense any unusual or irregular phenomena at the outer edge. You will feel a flow but when you feel a hole, prickles like a hedgehog, or bulge you will know something is wrong. You may feel heat or cold or electrical activity as different from the rest of the aura. You can ask questions about any emotional traumas or injuries but from scanning you will immediately feel what needs to be healed or what chakras are unbalanced.

You then simply open up and merge with the other body. You become that person and feel everything that she or he feels. If you merge gently and are very neutral the person will usually lower their defences. It is important not to be invasive and you will be able to sense the response and adjust it accordingly.

Bring your spirit back into your body. It won't be there long if your body is in pain so that is the benefit of clearing old pain pictures away. The body is a temple for the spirit. Offer spirit integration for harmony and mutual benefit. Cleaning up the energies so the connection can be realized will bring your miracles back home to you.

Other people's energy gets hooked into you by their criticizing, putting you down, making you feel inferior, not good enough, guilty, you do not have friends, you are not good enough, fat, ugly, etc. Their opinions are cords into your body from them to you. You did not sign up for slavery, so do not allow all their opinions to hook into you or bring you down. You are not their whipping post and slavery has been abolished!

Give the aura a psychic massage. Like you comb your hair comb out the aura which gives a calming effect. The chakras are delicate so you realign them. Is there any foreign energy in them? Sometimes you will see the punishment game, you punish them and they punish you back. If you invest in this game you exhaust your energy. You can laugh and watch the game without buying into it. Serious energy is like molasses and heavy. Serious energy gets stuck and is a lot of effort. Run your own energy and be in humour and amusement. Play and have fun and be simple.

Occasionally, a person makes a conscious decision not to be healed or not to hear something. If a person does not want a healing, they can reject it. This is always their choice and you can never force it on them. The resistance people have to the successful healing is that it changes their life and the way they view it. Their life is never the same after such a shift. Many who have held on to blame and been stuck in it suddenly see there is no one to blame. They have to take responsibility for their own actions and life. There are payoffs for victims and when they see they will have to change their ways (no more manipulation, poor-me, etc.) It is too comfortable for some and they do not want to change.

> Give your aura a psychic massage – it has a vastly calming effect

I gave a healing to a Katy who had learnt to be a master manipulator and controller. It had worked for her up till this time, but when she saw what it was doing to her she came clean and actually asked people not to allow her to manipulate them any more. Most did not know what she had been doing or what she was talking about. It was difficult but Katy just did not want to do it any more. She did not need to manipulate and control any more and it was a big relief to be honest. All that energy she had used could now be used for her creativity and fun.

One wealthy housewife in London insisted I heal her executive husband as he was stressed out and working too hard. Well, he insisted he did not believe in it at all but would go along with it for his wife to stop nagging him. The first two times he felt nothing. The third time he jumped up like a two-year-old. 'I can feel it, I can see it;' he shouted. He was so excited. His whole life has changed for the better.

By having the second chakra turned down to around 5 or 10% open while giving readings allows energy to be sensed while maintaining good boundaries and keeping your own energy set the way you like it.

Receiving a reading/healing

I became so excited the first time I had a psychic reading, because I came out of a dark cloud of confusion and stopped the wars in my energy field. Being validated for being psychic confirmed the people I grew up with were not psychic, and the confusion around this melted away. I could never understand why people would lie to me and expect me to believe them. When someone lies, there is the vibration or energy of what the person telling the lie is trying to make you believe about it. These are two completely separate things, and this is what creates confusion. To a psychic, you hear and see these two things at the same time.

The only good liar is the one who believes his or her own lies, so there is no difference between the two energies. This is what makes pathological liars and people without consciences so effective. We all hate lies but everything outside of you is a lie. It is someone else's reality, life experience, or will, outside of you. If you don't get too stuck on the emotion of this you can decide what to do with this piece of information. Do I leave it alone and leave or do I accept it as part of me?' As you find your own spiritual truth you decide what is true for you. You can look at something and read the truth of what you see.

In this decade we will all take responsibility and decide what is true for each of us, as governments will not be able to lie to you. Religious lies told during childhood will have no energy on you. The amazing thing is that you may find that your dearly beloved partner, even your own child, may in fact be your enemy and sabotaging all your mock-ups. You have been living with the enemy all along and you believed all the lies of affection and love whilst being sabotaged surreptitiously behind the scenes. Of course, this may not be the case. Truth is hard to face up to and look at, but when you come out of denial many things will surface that you wither in pain, sadness and agony about. That is the bad news, the good news is that it is so beneficial that you finally saw it and can move on to people who truly love and value you for who you are. The truth sets you free.

Having a healing is having a look at where you are and saying a 'hello' to Spirit. This is who you are. Here is some energy on the outside (foreign) not yours. You are a beautiful spirit. Say hello to pink energy, which is loving and caring. Black and grey are serious, so move them out.

Benefits you will gain from reading this book

You will have more energy and look and feel younger day by day.

You will appear radiant, calm, peaceful and neutral to anything anyone throws at you, be it abuse, their problems, opinions, judgements, punishment, jealously, you are less than, not good enough, stupid, poor, bad, etc.

You will learn to stay in your own energy, independent from other people's emotional state.

Your decisions will be clear and you will realize your dreams easily and effortlessly.

You will not take in other people's insanity, judgements and beliefs.

You will take back your power and affinity.

You will open up new doors for healthy and loving people to come into your life.

You will learn how to tell your energy from others.

You will open doors, allowing you to take control of your life and to create what you desire.

You will learn to trust your own information. This helps you to deal with difficult situations at work and in personal relationships.

You will get off the emotional roller coaster and identify your feelings and what is behind them and act appropriately.

You will understand the flood of visual information you receive, sort it out and use it in constructive ways.

You will create boundaries and get a better sense of who you are as a being, so you can clarify your desires and manifest them.

About the Author

Carmel Greenwood was born in Australia and left on her eighteenth birthday to discover the world. After travelling to Europe she went to Hong Kong for two weeks' holiday and stayed 28 years. She started out as a secretary, then became a stockbroker and finally ran her own financial investment company. After learning all about making money and making enough of it, she developed her healing abilities, wrote books and produced a *Go For Gold* series of healing videos and cassette tapes.

Carmel speaks regularly at schools and to young professional organizations as well as giving workshops around the world. She is also involved with Operation Smile (changing lives...one smile at a time) in Hong Kong and London. The proud mother of five children, she has been described in the press as `having an enormous, infectious guffaw that could coax the sun from the steeliest sky' and that she is someone who is `laughing her way to the top'.

Laughter and the ability not to take herself too seriously have enabled her to cope and survive difficult situations and survive triumphantly. For example, she watched her first marriage crumble in the face of her late ex-husband's chronic alcoholism. But she overcame this, marking her entry into the rank of world-class authors in 1991 with the completion of her book *Letting Go and Loving Life*. The latter explains how she transcended the experience of being a victim and moved to a place of personal power, creating a new reality for herself in joining the money-making business and starting her life afresh. Success and financial independence followed, only to have the life-shattering experience of her son, at twenty-one years, nearly dying from a drug overdose. Trying to cope with every mother's worst nightmare of dealing with her eldest daughter's and son's dependence on drugs resulted in mother and son penning *Wake Up Mum – Drugs Are Stealing Our Children*. This book is at once tender and gripping, but also a grim warning about a lifestyle that sees so many adolescents slip into the depths of heroin addiction. Mother and daughter are in the process of writing their story.

In 1993, Carmel and her family moved to San Francisco where she received a Certificate of Honor from the city's mayor, Willie Lewis Brown, Jr. 'for her work combatting drug problems in the community and improving the quality of life for children suffering from drug addictions.'

Carmel feels everyone has the ability to be happy and healthy. 'The only person that stands in your way is you. When you leave the past behind and live in the present you are free.' From living with the Aborigines in Australia as a child and experiencing their lifestyle she has been to Buckingham Palace with her husband to accept an award from the Queen. She now lives in London but feels equally at home in the USA, or indeed anywhere in the world. 'Home is where the heart is,' Carmel says, 'and I value every experience.'

Contact Carmel at:
Website: www.carmelconcepts.com
E-mail: carmelconcepts@ibm.net